GRACE
The Story of a Princess

PHYLLIDA HART-DAVIS

Willow Books
Collins
St. James's Place, London
1982

Acknowledgements
Michael Balfour Ltd and the publishers thank
the British Film Institute, London, for their
assistance with the preparation of research
material, and they thank the following for their
kind permission to reproduce the photographs
on these pages:
Michael Balfour Collection 10, 26, 31, 34, 35,
   39, 42, 141, 142
Camera Press 70, 101, 103, 124
John Finler 58
Fox Photos 64, 65, 77
John Hillelson 57, 74, 91, 99, 106, 107, 116, 118,
   119, 120, 121, 125
Kobal Collection 28/9, 32, 33, 36, 42, 43, 45, 59
Popperfoto 14, 18, 19, 20, 21, 24, 56, 57, 61, 63,
   76, 79, 88/9, 92, 98, 100, 133
Barrie Pattison 28, 40
Rex Features 70, 84, 90, 94, 95, 114, 122, 123,
   126, 127, 129, 130, 131, 135
Harry Smith Collection 6
Frank Spooner Pictures 66, 79, 85, 102, 106, 109,
   113, 126, 131, 132, 136/7, 138/9
Syndication International Cover, 2, 57, 86, 110,
   111
John Topham Picture Library 14, 16, 17, 21, 22,
   25, 32, 37, 44, 52, 54, 57, 60, 69, 73, 81, 83,
   88/9, 93, 96, 97, 104/5, 108, 117

Willow Books
William Collins Sons & Co Ltd
London Glasgow Sydney Auckland
Toronto Johannesburg

First published 1982

Hart-Davis, Phyllida
  Grace.
  1. Grace *Princess, Consort of Rainier, Prince of Monaco*
  1. Title
  944'. 949   DC 943.G7
    ISBN: 0-00-218089-8

This book was devised,
designed and produced by
Michael Balfour Ltd
3 Wedgwood Mews
Greek Street, London W1V 5LW
© Michael Balfour Ltd 1982
Text © Phyllida Hart-Davis 1982

Editor-in-Chief	Michael Balfour
Project Co-ordinator	Belinda Davies
Picture Research	Diane Rich
Design	Tom Deas / Rita Wüthrich
Typesetting	Project Reprographics Ltd
Reproduction	Colour Workshop Ltd
Printers	Development Workshop Ltd
Binders	The Garden City Press Ltd

Grace

The Story of a Princess

CONTENTS

The Life of Her Serene Highness Princess Grace

Grace de Monaco, a hybrid tea rose
introduced by Universal Rose Selection in 1956,
the year of her marriage

Her Serene Highness
Princess Grace of Monaco

12th November 1929 -
14th September 1982

"You're Sensational"

I have no proof,
When people say
You're more or less aloof,
That you're sensational.

"Sen-*sational* . . . sen-*sational*" went the refrain of the most haunting song that Cole Porter wrote for the film *High Society*; and although the words were intended for the movie's heroine, Tracy Lord, they applied perfectly to the actress who played her, Grace Kelly, then at the zenith of her fame and fortune.

She *was* sensational. To those who knew and worked with her, she was a magical person, a unique individual whose fascination has never been easily defined.

Her cool composure baffled the Hollywood publicity machine, which could only describe her as a snow-maiden, or as an ideal example of a clean, wholesome American girl "with stainless steel insides". But, in the words of Alfred Hitchcock, her great friend and mentor, she was a thrilling combination of "fire and ice", "fire burning in ice", a goddess who "exuded sexual elegance".

Her screen career was one of the most meteoric ever known. She soared up into the skies over Hollywood like a newly discovered comet, and less than five years later, of her own accord, she vanished from the film world's horizon, still blazing.

When she sailed for Europe and marriage to Prince Rainier, the car bearing Grace to the New York docks drove straight into a freight lift and was hoisted to the liner's sun-deck, to save her from the crowds. At a Press conference in the ship's observation lounge no less than 200 cameramen and reporters fought to get near her.

In Monaco she managed the transition from film star to Princess with the effortless ease of a true thoroughbred. As the years went by, her legendary looks scarcely changed. To one man who met her often in the Principality she was the most magnetic being imaginable. "When she came into a room, you looked at no-one else," he said. "Her beauty was breath-taking."

For quarter of a century Her Serene Highness served her adopted state with selfless devotion; yet only after her sudden death in September 1982 did her subjects realise how much they owed her, and how much they loved her. The shock of her death went around the world, and millions of her fans felt cruelly cheated by the fates which had prematurely cut down a woman of such goodness and such calm.

She will always be remembered and perhaps her countless admirers will agree that she can share an epitaph engraved on a wall in an English church for someone who died in the seventeenth century:

Know, Reader,

that if Piety Prudence Witt Innocence

or Beauty could rescue from the grave

Shee had been immortall

1
THE KELLYS OF PHILADELPHIA

GRACE PATRICIA KELLY was born on Friday, November 12th 1929, the third child of Mr. and Mrs. John B. Kelly.

Her grandfather, another John, was a farm boy from Co. Mayo, in Ireland, who sailed out to America in the 1860's and married a fellow-emigrant, Norah Costello. Together they raised a large family, many of whom became successful in their adopted land. It was as if the Irish energy and talent, which had been long suppressed and starved by successive famines and economic miseries in the Old Country, suddenly burst into flower in the New World. One of Grace's uncles, George Kelly, became a well-known playwright; another a vaudeville artist who, with his imitations of a judge sentencing prisoners, was considered "the funniest man in America". The eldest son, Patrick Henry, built his construction firm into a considerable business whose slogan "Brickwork by Kelly" adorned a large number of the city's walls.

Yet for all their success, prosperity and undoubted respectability, the Kelly family did not figure in Philadelphia's Social Register. The City of Brotherly Love, founded by the Quaker William Penn with the aim that all men should be free to worship as they wished, the first capital of the United States and home of the famous Liberty Bell whose ringing announced the adoption of the Declaration of Independence, was also jealous of its social exclusivity and slow to admit outsiders to its Assembly Rooms.

Not that the Kellys cared: their interests lay in practical achievement, both at work and in sport, rather than in frivolous social activity. Grace's father John, a handsome, competitive extrovert who began his career carrying bricks for his elder brother, built up his own business into a thriving concern. In sport, too, he was fired by an unquenchable will to win. By constant training on the Schuylkill River during evenings and weekends, he made himself a top-class sculler.

Nor was he a man to forget a grudge. In 1920, when the stewards of Henley-on-Thames' Royal Regatta, with classic arrogance, rejected his entry for the Diamond Sculls on the grounds that, having once worked with his hands, he was not a gentleman, he entered instead for the Antwerp Olympic Games a few weeks later, and defeated the new Henley champion. Four years later he again won the Olympic single sculls. Nor did the matter end there: coaching his son Jack, known as "Kell", from the age of seven, he built him into an international oarsman who revenged his father's rejection with two Henley victories in the Diamond Sculls a generation later.

Grace's mother, Margaret Majer, was of German ancestry, and an athlete in her own right. She became the first woman physical education instructor at the University of Pennsylvania, and her clear-cut, Nordic good looks also secured her a successful career as a model. After her marriage she devoted a great deal of time and energy to the Women's Medical Hospital and College in Philadelphia, leading a crusade for the right of women to work in medicine.

Physical fitness and excellence at sports were one

Eight month old Grace surveys the world from the safety of her cot at the Kelly family home in Philadelphia.

At the beach near the Kelly family holiday home at Ocean City, New Jersey, Grace and her elder sister Margaret (Peggy), building a sandcastle.

Aged two, Grace already knows how to produce a confident smile for the camera.

of the Kelly creeds, no less important to John and his wife than the old-fashioned virtues of thrift, self-discipline, and regular attendance at St. Bridget's Roman Catholic Church. As a girl Grace did not find it easy to communicate with her father, and sometimes wished she had been a boy. Yet later in life she was always thankful for the precepts which he instilled in her. "Never be one who takes and gives nothing in return," he would say. "Everything must be earned through hard work and sincerity." Even when she was young she realised what a strong character he was.

"He was a natural leader," she said later. "People had to follow him." One of her great strengths was that she learned his rules and never deviated from them. She looked back on him with affection as a fine gentleman — "a champion in every sense of the word."

The Kelly children led an active, competitive life, with summers at their holiday home on the New Jersey shore at Ocean City, and the rest of the year in their spacious, sprawling red-brick house and

large garden in Philadelphia. They all enjoyed swimming, tennis, rowing and regular workouts at the gym — except for their second daughter.

As a child, Grace was always less robust than her sisters Peggy and Lizanne or her husky brother Kell. A quiet, short-sighted little girl with long skinny legs, her honey-blonde, silky hair parted on the side and tied up with a ribbon, she suffered from hayfever and other respiratory troubles, so that she was often kept in bed, playing with her dolls, instead of joining in the other children's rumbustious games. Yet the enforced isolation never seemed to worry her: throughout her life she retained an enviable ability to be perfectly happy in her own company. Another result of her frequent colds was that her voice became tiresomely nasal — a defect which persisted until she took professional speech therapy. But even if she was, by Kelly standards, physically weak, she did inherit the family's basic natural athleticism: a good, keen swimmer, she also became a useful tennis player, as well as an able rider.

Growing up as they did during the Depression and Second World War, Grace and her sisters were taught by their mother to cook, sew, and manage money frugally: although their home life was secure, even prosperous, Mrs. Kelly grew her own vegetables, made the children help with the gardening, and encouraged them to sell flowers for charity. Sometimes — by Grace's own later admission — the flowers were stolen at night from neighbours' gardens and sold back to their unsuspecting owners! And yet, whatever its motives, this horticultural activity had a lasting result, for it planted in Grace a lifelong love of flowers.

Between the ages of six and fourteen she went to a local convent school, Ravenhill. She had scarcely arrived there when it became clear that she had an in-built passion for the stage. She first trod the boards as a six-year-old Virgin Mary, dressed in a flowing white robe, and made such an impact that she curtsied to a standing ovation. She was thrilled when Douglas Fairbanks Junior visited the family: "He kissed me goodnight. I was never going to wash again," she said.

Her next serious attack of stage fever came when she was eleven and cast in a production put on by the Academy Players of Philadelphia. When the actress taking the part of her mother forgot her lines, Grace was quick-witted enough to drop a handbag and while bending to recover it provided a rapid prompt. After that incident her father is said to have remarked, "We've got a trouper on our hands."

Leaving Ravenhill, Grace went on to Stevens Academy in Germantown. There her teachers were disappointed by her apparent lack of interest in

scholastic achievement: apart from enjoying English and history, she directed most of her energy to drama — and boys. She was very popular with boys. Even in her plump, bespectacled mid-teens, with a permanent snuffle, she apparently never lacked a date. The neighbours' sons vied for her attention, and, years later, in her *Book of Flowers,* Princess Grace of Monaco admitted to treasuring old dried flower corsages from her school dates.

Although the Kelly children's existences were centred on Philadelphia, their outlook was by no means parochial, and they took a particular interest in two girls who were their almost exact contemporaries: Princess Elizabeth and Princess Margaret,

At the Olympic village in Rome for the 1960 Olympics, where her brother Jack ''Kell'' Kelly, who had previously won twice at Henley Regatta, rowed in the Double Sculls.

As bridesmaid at the wedding of her sister Lizanne to Donald Caldwell Levine. They were married in St. Bridget's Roman Catholic Church, Philadelphia, in June 1955, where the Kelly family worshipped throughout Grace's childhood.

Leaving New York on the Constitution, *bound for her wedding to Prince Rainier III in Monaco. Grace and her mother wear identical fur coats against the April wind.*

Grace and her two sisters, Lizanne on the left and Peggy on the right.

three thousand miles away across the Atlantic. Grace, like many Americans, was fascinated by the English Royal family, and she avidly followed every move that was reported from Buckingham Palace, Windsor, Sandringham or Balmoral.

She made her first visit to England in the summer of 1947, when she was seventeen, and the whole family crossed the Atlantic to watch Kell row at Henley. They stayed in the old Red Lion hotel beside the bridge, and had the great satisfaction of seeing their entry win the Diamond Sculls by a distance — a feat which he repeated in 1949.

For the moment, however, drama remained her central interest. When she was seventeen, she graduated from Stevens Academy where a classmate had written beneath her picture the prophetic announcement, "She is very likely to become a stage or screen star."

Still quiet — for a Kelly — still shy and unsure of herself, she spent much of her time composing amusingly individual verse:

> *I hate to see the sun go down*
> *And squeeze itself into the ground,*
> *Since one warm night it might get stuck*
> *And in the morning not get up.*

She wrote this at the age of fourteen. Though in home theatricals organised by her sister Peggy, two years her senior, Grace was usually denied a starring role, she took part with enthusiasm and also learned Shakespeare's Sonnets by heart for the sheer

19

Waving farewell to the thousands of New Yorkers who came to watch her departure for her wedding. So great was the crowd that Grace was whisked aboard the boat in a freight lift!

Eighty members of the Kelly clan and friends travelled with Grace to Monaco for the wedding. Together they presented a private cinema to the Palace as a wedding gift.

pleasure of hearing the words.

When she applied to enter Bennington College, however, she received a setback: she failed in maths. Instead, possibly influenced by the success of her playwright uncle George, her ambitions turned more directly towards the stage, and she applied to the American Academy of Dramatic Arts in New York, was auditioned and accepted.

Her immediate family was not enthusiastic. Her father had a poor opinion of the acting profession — a mistrust that extended to most intellectuals and artists — but then his daughter Grace had always been a mystery to him. Being himself so energetic and outgoing, he found it hard to understand a daughter who enjoyed sitting still, reading or writing. Margaret Kelly naturally worried about the precarious nature of a show-business career and the dangers lurking in wait for an innocent girl in New York. But if there was one characteristic more than any other that Grace had inherited from both her parents, it was steely determination. Now — as at every stage of her life — she knew what she wanted, and pursued it in a most determined fashion.

Standing beside the bust erected in memory of her father John B. Kelly in 1961. Left to right: Margaret Kelly (Grace's mother), the sculptor Reginald Beauchane, Princess Grace and Prince Rainier.

2
THE EARLY YEARS

After reluctantly agreeing that Grace might go to the American Academy of Dramatic Arts for a trial year, her parents set about finding her a room in the one place in New York where an out-of-town mother might then have felt sure her daughter was safe: the Barbizon Hotel.

In the late 1940's the Barbizon was one of those comforting anachronisms that actually worked: a hotel for single women to which men were denied access except with a pass and special permission. It had shops, hairdressers, a beauty parlour, a swimming pool — everything a girl might want. Quiet Grace Kelly, with her neat clothes, white gloves and beautiful blue eyes camouflaged by no-nonsense spectacles, slipped into a niche and felt immediately at home.

New York was a revelation to her — and a liberation. Away from the overwhelming presence of her family, she began to develop her own personality, to put together the ''Grace Kelly look'' which was to become her hallmark.

She loved the Academy and worked hard there, using the establishment's pre-Stanislavsky techniques to get inside her parts. One day she might be sent to study a real, live drunk, then come back and play the role. Another time, to her astonishment, she was packed off to the zoo to take minute observations of the gait and habits of a llama. She learnt to

Working as a model during her years at the American Academy of Dramatic Art in New York. Grace was soon earning over $400 a week, advertising a wide range of products.

walk on stage, and concentrated on lowering her voice.

For the convenience of students forced to help their finances with part-time jobs, the school work was divided into two four-hour shifts. Grace, though financially secure thanks to her parents, nevertheless took up modelling to fill the empty hours, and was soon earning $400 a week posing for advertisements for a variety of products, from Electrolux gadgets to Old Gold tobacco. She was a photographer's dream: patient, accommodating, with good bone structure, flawless skin, and an equable temperament. She was always punctual, always polite — the epitome of American womanhood, every father's ideal daughter. If she lacked anything, it was sex-appeal: to quote Ruzzie Green, the photographer, she was ''What we call 'nice clean stuff' in our business. She's not a top model and never will be. She's the girl next door. No glamour, no oomph, no cheesecake. . .''

Grace's image, indeed, was distinctly sedate. She wore well-cut suits and court shoes, white gloves and hats with little veils. All this went down well in the world of advertising; but when, on leaving stage school, she began the rounds of the casting offices, it was another story. Directors found her difficult to typecast. As she herself once said, she fell into the ''Too'' category — too tall, too leggy, too chinny. She read for thirty-eight parts without getting one. The constant rejections must have been dispiriting, but she never seems to have considered giving up. She went on doggedly making the rounds, and taking ballet and voice-production lessons.

She had also begun to attend Sanford Meisner's classes at the Neighbourhood Playhouse. One day

Twentieth-Century Fox telephoned her agent to ask if she would hurry to an immediate interview with the Hungarian director Gregory Ratoff, who was casting for the film *Taxi*. With no time to change, she felt horribly out of place among the other hopefuls in their studied makeup and high heels, but Ratoff was instantly taken by her unfashionable appearance. In Grace he saw just the raw material he needed for the immigrant Irish girl who enchants a tough New York cabbie. As she entered his office he threw up his arms and screamed, ''She's perfect! What I love about *this* girl is, she's not pretty!'' After assuring him she could speak with an Irish accent, she went home and worked hard at a brogue. She even tested for the film, but the part eventually went to another actress with more authentically Celtic looks.

All the same, jobs began to come thick and fast: she played in television shows and commercials and took minor parts in a summer repertory season, notably her uncle George's comedy *The Torchbearers* at the Bucks County Playhouse. Her first film role was in *Fourteen Hours* (1951), a thriller in which, as a young woman beset by marital problems, she discusses divorce with a lawyer while watching a real life drama across the street, where a would-be suicide, crouched on a ledge, threatens to jump.

Her first major break came in November 1949, at the age of twenty, when she opened at the Cort Theatre on Broadway in Strindberg's *The Father* — the grimly powerful story of a Swedish cavalry officer whose marriage eventually sends him mad. The English actor Raymond Massey was in the title role, and Grace, as his devoted daughter, attracted favourable comment from the critics. Though the play closed after sixty-nine performances, Massey thought highly of this *ingenue* and later remarked: ''Some actors have that quality. . . I have never been so impressed with anyone at first sight as I was with this girl. She had serenity. . .''

The time seemed ripe to launch out from the Barbizon into an apartment of her own. Grace moved to 9A, Manhattan House on 66th Street and 3rd Avenue. She furnished it with the excitement of a girl setting up house for the first time, and installed a parakeet called Henry. Here she could entertain her friends and feel at home without the benevolent despotism of the Barbizon's rules against boyfriends and electrical appliances.

Another nudge towards the Big Time came from her new agent, Edith van Cleve, of the Music Corporation of America, a shrewd and strong-minded lady who quickly recognised her new protégée's potential. She took a gamble that might easily have misfired but in the event paid off handsomely. The young actress was suddenly offered two conflicting engagements: to fly to Hollywood to play in an experimental Western, *High Noon* (1952), or to join the Elitch's Garden Theatre in Denver, Colorado, for a season of summer stock. Though the Hollywood offer was worth $750 a week, and the one from the theatre a mere $150, Edith advised Grace to go to Denver for the experience, and without hesitation Grace agreed. The calculated risk came off. As Edith had anticipated, the film fell behind schedule, so that when shooting finally started in September, Grace Kelly was still able to accept a part in the film which proved a thrilling turning point in her fledgling career.

One of the first film portraits of Grace, taken for her screen debut in Fourteen Hours, *a drama about a woman who watches from a lawyer's office as a suicide prepares to jump from a ledge across the street.*

At ease in the sun, the young actress on her way to the top.

*A strangely perceptive portrait by Cecil Beaton. She is asking
the camera a question, but what was it?*

3
GRACE KELLY

Now Hollywood had cast a lure over Grace for the third time. Once before, and then again after she left the Dramatic Academy, she had been offered parts in films but each time she had refused, feeling that she needed more acting experience. She was reluctant to become just another starlet in the Hollywood system. But the chance to play opposite Gary Cooper and be directed by the legendary Fred Zinnemann was too good to turn down.

It is the story of Sheriff Kane (Gary Cooper) who vows to rid his shabby frontier town of lawlessness. The task completed, he prepares to drive out of Hadleyville to honeymoon with his young bride when word reaches him that a convict, whom he helped to put behind bars five years earlier, is on the loose again, with three henchmen. Despite the pleas of his bride, Kane turns back to face the killers who are out for his blood. The men of the town who had promised to help him melt into the shadows like frightened rats; alone, as the hands of the clocks jerk towards high noon, the Sheriff walks stiff-legged down the centre of the empty dust street, to the saloon where the gunmen are waiting.

High Noon made a superb starring vehicle for Gary Cooper. His strong, silent character was perfect for the role. As his bride, whose Quaker upbringing makes her abhor violence, so that only at the last moment can she nerve herself to draw a gun and save her man, Grace Kelly had a difficult part to play. Her naturally composed and regal expression

Her ice-cool beauty was a phenomenon which Hollywood could not at first understand.

did not adapt easily to looking scared or pleading, and her performance was not in the same league as Cooper's. What was more, she knew it: being ruthlessly honest about her own abilities, she did not rate her achievement very highly.

But "Everything's so clear working with Gary Cooper," she said. "When I look into his face, I can see everything he's thinking. But when I look into my own face I see absolutely nothing. I *know* what I'm thinking, but it just doesn't show. I wonder if I'm ever going to be any good. Maybe I'd better go back to New York and make my face show."

Such candid objectivity was rare among actresses of that era. But then, as everyone who met Grace recognised, she was certainly no ordinary actress. As Jay Kanter, MCA's talent-spotter, remembered: "Just meeting her for the first time was quite an experience. She seemed to have it there in one look."

Nor did she allow the celebrated Hollywood razzamatazz — the Treatment — to overwhelm her. On the contrary. At her parents' suggestion, both her sisters accompanied her to the West Coast, and the three installed themselves in the comfort and glamour of the Chateau Marmont, then the epicentre of Hollywood activity. Famous stars of the time drank, and gossiped convivially, in its huge baroque bar, while hopeful newcomers flaunted their curves beside the swimming pool.

Life fell quickly into a routine for the Kelly sisters. They would rise early, check that Grace had her lines word perfect, and drive her out to the MGM studio for the day's shooting, from which they would collect her at tea-time. Dinner together would be followed by an intensive line-learning session and early bed. Seldom can Hollywood have had in its grasp such a hardworking and punctilious star.

The trouble was that it hardly knew what to do with her. Sexpots with pouting mouths and bulging bosoms, who stripped at the least provocation, were what Hollywood seemed to understand. A serious and beautiful actress who refused point blank to indulge in cheap publicity stunts, who even drew the line at appearing in a bathing dress, baffled MGM. The company had no idea how to publicise, or indeed cope with, somebody so intelligent and dignified.

She would not allow her measurements to appear on publicity handouts, and she was careful always to bring an extra girl along on any date in order to frustrate Hollywood gossip. It is hardly surprising, in retrospect, that Grace never felt at ease in the film capital, and always returned with relief to New York after working there. When *High Noon* was completed, the Kelly girls left the West Coast without delay and Grace was soon happily back in her little apartment with her pet parakeet, looking again for work in the theatre.

Despite her dissatisfaction with her own acting in *High Noon*, the film was a big success. It was awarded four Oscars, including the Best Scoring of a Drama; the Best Song (for the famous theme tune ''Do Not Forsake Me, Oh My Darling'' by Dimitri Tiomkin) and the Best Film Editing. Gary Cooper was voted the Best Actor of 1952 by the Academy of Motion Picture Arts. The result of these successes

High Noon: *Left to right — Lloyd Bridges, Katy Jurado, Gary Cooper and Grace Kelly.*

A poster for her first Hitchcock thriller, Dial M for
Murder: *The hired killer attacks the unsuspecting Grace as
she telephones her treacherous husband.*

was a new offer from MGM for a remake of a 1932 movie, *Red Dust*, to be updated, rescripted, and moved from the original location in Indo-China to East Africa. The new director was John Ford.

Although Grace had formerly refused to be tied down to a long contract, this time she accepted MGM's seven-year offer of $750 a week, provided she was allowed a year off every two years to go back to the legitimate theatre in New York. After some haggling, MGM agreed and the contract was signed. Her reasons for tackling this new challenge were, as she explained, three-fold: John Ford, Clark Gable, and a free trip to Africa.

As always, her priorities were clear; she knew exactly where her career was going, and she prepared for the trip with her usual thoroughness. Her co-stars, Ava Gardner, Clark Gable, and Donald Sinden met her at Zurich. They were astonished to find her, as the film's publicist put it, "lovely, blonde and composed, reading quietly in the airport terminal lobby. The book, as I recall, was one dealing with the experiences of an African white hunter."

She had done her homework with a thoroughness that startled her fellow-actors. Donald Sinden, who found her "demure and amazingly pretty", included a charming anecdote in his book *A Touch of the Memoirs*. On their first night at the New Stanley Hotel in Nairobi, he, she and Clark Gable sat down to dinner together:

"Our waiter was a Kikuyu and Grace proceeded to astonish Clark and me by ordering the entire

Camp life on the greatest ever safari — Hollywood style.
Mogambo *was filmed on location in kenya, Uganda and*
Tanganyika (now Tanzania).

A sharp contrast with the sultry beauty of Ava Gardner,
Grace played the cool English wife, whose passion is aroused
by a White Hunter, Clark Gable.

meal for the three of us in Swahili. . . Having served the coffee, the waiter was just moving away when Grace called after him, '*Lete, ndizi, tafadhali.*' By then we had learned that *lete* meant 'bring' and *tafadhali* meant 'please', but Clark, with some incredulousness, asked her, 'What's an *ndizi*?' ·

Before she could reply, the waiter has turned and in a bored American accent answered, 'It's a banana,' and wearily made his way.''

During all the weeks she spent on location in Kenya, Uganda and Tanganyika (now Tanzania), Grace never wasted a moment. Always she was looking around, learning new facts, picking up background knowledge. In strong contrast with the newly-married Ava Gardner and Frank Sinatra (who chafed at the need to live under canvas with such a beautiful and temperamental wife, tormented by insects, and loathing the heat) she profited by every minute in Africa.

The story of *Red Dust*, now retitled *Mogambo* (1953) — which means 'passion' in Kiswahili — concerns Victor, a White Hunter (Gable) whose dalliance with Honey Bear, (Ava Gardner), an American entertainer who has come on safari to get away from it all, is interrupted by the arrival in their camp of an English anthropologist (Donald Sinden) and his beautiful, supposedly-frigid wife Linda (Grace). The Englishwoman's cool facade melts as she and the White Hunter become aware of their passion; though her husband is too obtuse to notice the change in her, Honey Bear spots it at once and jealously tries to alert him to the danger threatening his marriage.

There is a dramatic scene between the two men when Victor wrestles with his conscience about whether to rescue his beloved's husband from a gorilla, or leave him to die so that she will be free to marry him. In the end he does the right thing: kills the gorilla, and destroys his own chance of happiness by telling Linda that he was only amusing himself with her. As the British couple go on their way, Victor turns once more to Honey Bear.

It was a film safari in true Hollywood style. Even now, thirty years later, Nairobi remembers the immensity of the preparations and the departure of eight white hunters, 175 whites and 300 blacks on location. The safari camp was equipped with everything it could possibly have needed, including a hospital and mobile cinema. An air-strip was cleared for supply-planes to land, and special guards were hired to protect the whole complex and its denizens from the Mau Mau gangs then terrorising the White Highlands.

While Ava Gardner and Frank Sinatra remained in camp, drinking, quarrelling and making it up

An early screen kiss: Grace and Robert Cummins in Dial M for Murder.

with the maximum noise and drama, Grace seized the opportunity to see as much as she could of this strange and magnificent continent. With Clark Gable and ''Bunny'' Allen, a white hunter proficient in handling film stars, she would get up in that magic hour before dawn when the animals are returning from their night's hunting beneath the wide, primrose-and-pink streaked sky, and jolt in a hard-sprung Land Rover across the plains.

From the first she hit it off with four-times-married Clark Gable, though they both studiously sidestepped any suggestion of romance. It seems that they simply enjoyed one another's company. No doubt this connoisseur of beautiful women admired Grace's looks; but he must also have appreciated his co-star's keen intelligence and interest in everything new, besides the Kelly toughness which scorned minor discomforts such as heat, thorns and the richly-varied insect life. On her side, Grace clearly warmed to his charm and sophistication, as well as respecting his professional skill. While anxious columnists in Europe cabled demands for confirmation or denial of a romance between them, Gable and Kelly just laughed.

Impervious to the wonders of Africa all around them, Ava and Frank did their best to keep the ball rolling in camp with a series of celebrations. Her birthday, Gable's birthday, their first wedding anniversary, Frank's securing of the role he coveted in *From Here to Eternity* — all were occasions for corks to pop and sparks to fly between the exhibitionist Ava and her nervously excitable husband. Though Grace was sorry to leave Africa, Ava could hardly

wait to get back to the bright lights.

When the final scenes for the film were shot at Elstree, in England, Grace met Donald Sinden's wife Diana, and was enchanted by their small son Jeremy, then two-and-a-half. "She looked at him with absolute *envy*," Sinden remembers. "It was obvious that she was determined to get married and have a family of her own one day."

Mogambo received mixed reviews. Though the critics agreed that the scenery was magnificent and the animals superbly photographed, the actors' performances were not so generally admired. The best

that the *Daily Telegraph's* Campbell Dixon could say was that "Miss Gardner acts bravely. The best of the other performances are those of Philip Dainton as the nice White Hunter, and the father gorilla we see defending his family — though of course the gorilla has an unfair advantage in the matter of dialogue."

Newsweek was more enthusiastic: "Grace Kelly makes one of the loveliest patricians to appear on the screen in a long time. Her particular quality is the suggestion that she is well born without being arrogant, cultivated without being stuffy, and

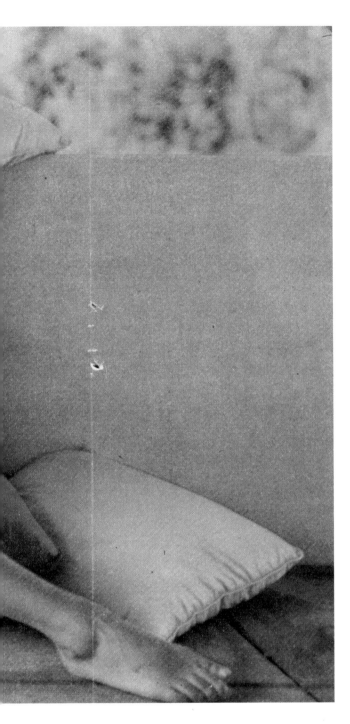

Grace Kelly (1955)

highly-charged emotionally without being blatant.'' *Look* magazine named her the Best Actress of 1953, and the film proved a financial success, grossing close to $5 million. No-one disputed the fact that Grace's visit to Africa gave her new poise and self-confidence. MGM's technicians had done as much for her looks as John Ford's direction did for her technique, and she was a fast learner.

As she was now under contract to MGM she did not immediately return to New York, but rented an apartment on Sweetzer Street in North Hollywood; she shared it with another actress, Rita Gam, besides her secretary Prudence Wise. The girls became great friends, sharing diets and boyfriends and keeping the icebox well stocked with champagne. Yet there was always a temporary air about their living arrangements: people said it was as if Grace had her bags packed all the time, ready to fly off to New York.

On this second visit to the film capital, she guarded her reputation as vigilantly as ever. She still took girlfriends with her on dates, showed no interest in the Hollywood way of life, and whipped on her spectacles to discourage would-be wolves. As a friend put it when asked for a Grace Kelly anecdote: ''I don't

think Grace would allow an anecdote to happen to her.'' But though she was the despair of publicity men, people who mattered much more were observing her career with interest. Among them was Alfred Hitchcock.

She returned to New York and accepted the leading role in *The Moon is Blue*, which was to be staged in Philadelphia's Playhouse in the Park. Rather unexpectedly, this theatre was one of her father's pet projects. During the run she was telephoned by Jay Kanter of MCA with the news that Warner Brothers were negotiating to hire her from MGM for a fee of $20,000 in order to co-star her with Ray Milland in *Dial M for Murder* (1954). This was a thriller, scripted from Frederick Knott's play, to be directed by Hitchcock. He had seen her *Taxi* screen test, and what had struck him was her potential for restraint. As he explained: ''I always tell actors, 'Don't use the face for nothing. Don't start scribbling over the sheet of paper until we have something to write. We may need it later.' Grace has this control. It's a rare thing for a girl at such an age.''

Another director, George Seaton, corroborated: ''Grace doesn't throw everything at you in the first

Grace and James Stewart in Rear Window. *As her chairbound fiancé watches his neighbours, he begins to suspect a murder has been committed.*

five seconds. Some girls give you everything they've got at once, and there it is — there is no more. But Grace is like a kaleidoscope: one twist, and you get a whole new facet.''

Hitchcock's faith was justified. Her performance in *Dial M for Murder* far surpassed any of her earlier roles; her ability to act with her head as well as her body was at last given a chance to shine through.

The story is a complicated one of deceit and suspense — a typical Hitchcock subject. Tony (Ray Milland), jealous husband of a rich wife, Margot (Grace), hires a killer (Anthony Dawson) to strangle her when he is away among friends who can provide an alibi. He telephones to draw Margot to the telephone and present the killer with a tethered target.

When she picks up the receiver, Tony says nothing, but waits to listen to the murderer's attack. Margot, however, seizes the desk scissors and stabs her assailant. As he lies dead at her feet she picks up the telephone to summon the police. Tony answers.

In Rear Window, *Grace gave her audience a hint of fire beneath the cool exterior.*

She begs him to hurry home: she has been attacked. When she tells him she has killed the attacker, he claims that the man was her lover and that she murdered him during a quarrel.

There are many twists and turns before Tony's treachery is uncovered by the police inspector who discovers the existence of a duplicate key to the apartment.

The *New York Times* liked the film very much. "In the pliant hands of Alfred Hitchcock, past master of the job of squeezing thrills, the coils twine with sleek and silken evil." The same critic declared that Grace "does a nice job of acting the wife's bewilderment, terror, and grief." *The Daily Telegraph* went further:

"Ray Milland plays the husband with a fine, hard polish; Grace Kelly, accused by Americans of being too 'English' (in an English part), is lovely and agreeably restrained. . . All things considered, *Dial M for Murder* is one of the most polished thrillers we have had in years."

Under Hitchcock's direction, Grace's acting had acquired a new flexibility. He encouraged her to pitch her voice lower, and at last the emotions which had previously been concealed under that fine-boned exterior began to be seen in her face.

But despite the impressive blossoming of her film career, theatre remained her first love, and she was disappointed not to win the role of Roxanne in *Cyrano de Bergerac*, with José Ferrer, although she read for it twice.

This setback was soon forgotten in the excitement of a new invitation from Hitchcock to star opposite James Stewart in a thriller for Paramount called *Rear Window* (1954). Once again, with fate on her side, Grace hit a jackpot.

Lisa, a photographer's model helping her temporarily chair-bound fiancé pass the time as his broken leg mends, is drawn into the mystery of the behaviour of Jeff's neighbours, whose voices he can hear and whose actions he can observe from the window by which he sits.

The invalid wife nags her husband Lars continuously. His restraint in answering sounds saintly. But Jeff's suspicions are aroused when a sudden silence falls. Later he sees Lars carrying a suitcase that is obviously heavy, and still later observes the

nagging wife's dog, lowered to the ground in a basket at appropriate intervals, sniffing and scratching in a flower bed.

When Lars is out and Jeff watching for his return, Lisa slips across to investigate and discovers a woman's wedding ring, which she removes as evidence. Suspense mounts as Jeff sees Lars returning while the oblivious Lisa is still searching his apartment. . .

Rear Window confirmed Grace Kelly as a box-office draw in her own right. Cinemas showing the film omitted the names of Hitchcock and Stewart from their hoardings and advertised merely "Grace Kelly in *Rear Window*." As Frank Scully remarked in his column for *Variety*, "Never have I watched a girl climb upward with such undiminished power, unaided by scandal or any other agencies of the sort of notoriety that the modern world too frequently confuses with fame.

"Up to *Rear Window* she seems to have done it wholly on her merits as a lady. In that one an attempt was made to show she had some of the more

Green Fire was a typical Hollywood mishmash of adventure and romance about emerald hunting in South America.

Cover girl

flagrant forms of sex appeal as well as rarer talents."

Scully was not alone in his surprise at finding that Grace could give a performance as provocative as it was understated. As Hitchcock said, she exuded "sexual elegance", which made every movement, every phrase, an invitation and a challenge to every male in her audience, while she remained perfectly well-bred, every inch a lady. It knocked critics for six to see the girl they had classified as a remote, touch-me-not goddess extract a flimsy nightie from her handbag and, putting it on, announce to her chair-bound fiancé, 'Preview of coming attractions.'

To quote Hitchcock again, "Sex on the screen should be suspenseful, I feel. If sex is too blatant or obvious, there's no suspense. We're after the drawing-room type, the real ladies, who become

The Country Girl shows Grace in a different light: as the downtrodden, dowdy wife of an alcoholic. Her performance won her The Academy Award as Best Actress of 1954.

whores once they're in the bedroom. Poor Marilyn Monroe had sex written all over her face, and Brigitte Bardot isn't very subtle either.''

Grace's appeal was very subtle, very elegant: to a film public which had become punch-drunk with what Van Johnson wittily called ''a broadside of broads'', her cool charm, with its undertones of hidden fire, was a welcome and refreshing change. They flocked to see her.

With a jolt, MGM woke up to the fact that the unusual young actress they had under contract was a very hot property indeed, and that if they made no use of her, others would. Too late they cast around for a suitable vehicle for their new star: before they could come up with anything, Grace started work again for Paramount, this time in a war film called *The Bridges at Toko-Ri* (1954).

Based on a novel by James Michener, directed by Mark Robson and produced jointly by George Seaton and William Perlberg, this was a story with a principally male appeal and gave Grace little chance

to show her star quality. Yet like all her leading men, William Holden, who played Lieut. Harry Brubaker, a jet pilot entrusted with the mission of destroying strategic supply bridges during the Korean War, was instantly captivated by her blend of beauty, brains and professionalism. As he said, ''With some actresses, you have to keep snapping them to attention like a puppy. Grace is always concentrating. In fact she sometimes keeps me on track.'' This, from one of Hollywood's ablest professionals, was praise worth having.

As Nancy Brubaker, Harry's wife, Grace played the part of a woman in desperate fear for her husband's life, yet putting on a brave face for him and their daughters when she spends a last week with him in Tokyo before he flies out on his kamikaze mission. For the first time on film she was seen in a suitably demure swimsuit; another break-through was to show her in bed with a man — her husband in the film, admittedly, but all the same a scene at which she might well have baulked two years previously.

Although it was a run-of-the-mill film, her performance again pleased the critics. The *New York Times* called her "briefly bewitching", and the *New York Herald-Tribune* agreed that "Everyone knows how nice it is to have her around." But Grace was eager to get her teeth into a part that would really show her mettle, and for the first time in her film career she made it perfectly plain that she was determined to have one particular role — that of Georgie Elgin in *The Country Girl* (1954).

The trouble was, a lot of big names among Hollywood actresses also coveted the part, and MGM were reluctant to loan Grace Kelly out to Paramount again. The bush telegraph hummed with rumour, speculation and gossip. The co-directors, Seaton and Perlberg, were besieged with invitations and propositions. The role had fallen vacant only because the actress Jennifer Jones was pregnant and unable to act in the film. Seaton and Perlberg, delighted with the way Grace had worked for them in *The Bridges at Toko-Ri*, wanted her to have the part, but the problem of getting MGM to release her seemed insuperable. Another major difficulty was opposition from Bing Crosby, who had the male lead. Not surprisingly, knowing the roles she had played so far, he could not see Grace as the dowdy, frumpish wife of an alcoholic, and he was resolutely opposed to having her star with him.

Grace, however, had one trump card in her hand, and now she slapped it down on the table. She threatened to leave films altogether and go back to the New York theatre, unless MGM released her to Paramount. There was no doubt that she meant it. The MGM hierarchy was forced to recognise the unpalatable fact that they needed her a good deal more than she needed them: reluctantly they agreed to a deal by which Paramount was to pay them $50,000 for her services, plus a penalty fee for every day they retained her after the date when shooting was to start for MGM's own Grace Kelly vehicle, *Green Fire* (1954). In addition, she was bound to make another film for her home company before taking on work for anyone else.

After suitable haggling, negotiations were completed, and the only remaining problem was to win round Bing Crosby. This she managed in record time: after a single week's shooting on *The Country Girl*, Bing remarked to his director with typical generosity, "Never let me open my big mouth again. This girl can really act."

The screenplay of *The Country Girl* was adapted by

With William Holden in The Bridges at Toko-Ri *in which she played a wife whose pilot husband is sent on a kamikaze mission.*

George Seaton from a play by Clifford Odets. It is the story of Frank Elgin (Crosby), a singer and actor who turns to drink as his career sinks into the doldrums. When a Broadway director, Bernie Dodd (William Holden), offers him a come-back, Frank blames his decline on his wife Georgie (Grace), and says that only if he can get away from her influence will he regain his old powers.

Bernie, taken in by this, tries to separate the couple: only when she makes him see that Frank has chosen alcohol to help him deaden the guilt he feels over the death of his son, who was killed by a car, does Bernie realise that it is Georgie who has supported her husband all along and has prevented his complete disintegration. He also realises that he loves her. Together they work to rebuild Frank's confidence and make his come-back a success. When it is clear that Frank is capable of standing on his own once more, Bernie tries to persuade Georgie to leave him, but although she longs to, she refuses, and pledges herself to stay with Frank, who never knows how near his wife and friend came to betraying him.

In the role of the dowdy, loyal Georgie, worn out by years of supporting a weak, self-centred husband, Grace achieved a performance that outshone all earlier ones. Not only did she transform her physical

The new Hitchcock extravaganza, To Catch A Thief *was set on the French Riviera.*

appearance; she also projected a mental attitude that was the very reverse of her intensely positive self.

Instead of brimming with vitality, she looked drained, exhausted. She slouched, she sprawled; dressed in a baggy cardigan and seated skirt, with spectacles pushed up on a head of dull, greasy hair, she looked like a woman at the limit of her resources. But she played the love scenes with a compassion and poignancy that astonished everyone on the set. The glossy image was gone, and in its place she revealed depths no-one had suspected: small wonder that when shooting ended the entire company presented her with a plaque inscribed *"This will hold you until you get next year's Academy Award."*

The film was well received. *Look* magazine wrote: "Crosby and Miss Kelly play this human tragedy with a compassion and psychological insight reaching the best traditions of dramatic skill." *Cue* was even more fulsome: "The Crosby-Kelly-Holden team comes just about as close to theatrical perfection as we are likely to see on-screen in our time." The picture made more than six million dollars for Paramount: better still, it justified the company's

With Cary Grant on the Moyenne Corniche in a scene from To Catch A Thief. *Monte Carlo harbour lies below, with the Palace dominating the headland beyond.*

Once again she took to the water in To Catch A Thief.

Alfred Hitchcock was the first to realise Grace's potential for "sexual elegance". He directed her in three pictures and became a great friend.

With Cary Grant who played a retired jewel thief determined to protect his reputation.

testimonial plaque. Grace Kelly was nominated for an Oscar on the strength of her role.

Competition was fierce that year. Judy Garland was front-runner for the Actress of the Year Award for her performance in *A Star is Born*. At the hospital where she was recuperating from the birth of her son, cameras were ready to switch onto her as the awards were announced. When William Holden, the presenter, handed the bronze statuette to Grace instead, Sid Luft is said to have comforted his wife with the words: "Baby, — the Academy Awards: you've got yours in the incubator!"

This was the peak of Grace's film career, proving once and for all that she was not only beautiful but an outstanding actress as well. But now MGM claimed its pound of flesh: after such dramatic heights, *Green Fire,* their projected film about emerald-mining in South America, was almost bound to be an anticlimax, and so it proved.

Polite and professional as always, Grace fulfilled her obligation to the company by playing opposite Stewart Granger in this typically-Hollywood mishmash of romance and adventure, but neither of them enjoyed the location work and neither was happy with the finished product. When, with amazing crassness, the studio caused a cut-out of Grace's head on a bosomy body in a clinging, green, strapless gown to be exhibited outside the Broadway Theatre, she altered her daily perambulations to avoid passing the spot. "It makes me so mad," she declared in a rare outburst of annoyance. "And the dress isn't even in the picture!"

Green Fire did no-one much good, and it wreaked further havoc in Grace's relations with MGM, making her even more wary of their next offering. She turned down *The Cobweb* (as did Lana Turner) and after reading the script of *Quentin Durward* she rejected it too, with the eminently reasonable explanation that "all the men can duel and fight, but all I'd have to do would be to wear thirty-five different costumes, look pretty and frightened. . The stage directions on every page say 'She clutches her jewel box and flees.' I just thought I'd be bored."

Grace's magnificent costumes in To Catch A Thief *were created by Helen Rose who later designed her wedding dress.*

Three other scripts (*Diane, Something of Value,* and *Bannon*) she also turned down, and eventually, after she had refused yet another assignment, (to play opposite Spencer Tracy in a Western called *Jeremy Rodrock* which was finally released under the title *Tribute to a Bad Man*), MGM suspended her.

Grace explained to the Press: "It's my first experience with a thing like this, and I guess there's nothing I can do but sit here and wait till they want me back. I feel very strange not getting a salary any more."

When pressed for her reasons for rejecting the chance to co-star with Spencer Tracy, one of Hollywood's biggest box-office draws, she enlarged: "I felt I had to turn down the roles because they're just parts that I couldn't see myself playing. I hope they're not too mad at me. Perhaps I was spoilt by my loan-out pictures. Now Metro say that they won't lend me to other studios any more. They feel that it's time I made one for them — and of course they have a good talking-point."

What she did not add, but what everyone who heard her must have realised, was that MGM's handling of her career had been continuously inept. Of the six films she had made while under contract to them, only two, and those the least successful, had been for her home studio. Finding that she would not conform to their preconceived ideas, they had made no effort to give her work that would suit her unique looks and individual talent. If it had not been for Hitchcock and the Perlberg-Seaton team, her career in films would have been undistinguished. *Time* magazine produced a telling phrase when it described Hollywood as being "eager to adopt Actress Kelly, white gloves and all," and "trying hard, with the air of an ill-at-ease lumberjack worrying whether he is using the right spoon."

Once again, as her future hung in the balance, Hitchcock waddled to the rescue. He wanted her for a new thriller set on the French Riviera, *To Catch a Thief* (1955). Cary Grant was already signed up, and the role of the rich, haughty American beauty who falls for the charm of a cracksman looked perfect for Grace. Delicate negotiations were set in train between MGM and Paramount, and after some hard bargaining, agreement was reached. Paramount was to be allowed to "borrow" Grace for the fourth time on condition that they released William Holden for a film which MGM was about to schedule. Once again her brilliantly gifted champion had snatched Grace from the dragon's jaws. . . but this time with dramatic and far-reaching consequences.

In contrast to the restrained, restricted domestic backgrounds and understated clothes of *Dial M for Murder* and *Rear Window, To Catch a Thief* was to be a

In The Swan, *she played Princess Alexandra, daughter of an impoverished noble house, who is pressed by her family to marry a rich Prince many years her senior. Here she looks wistfully away from her handsome tutor, Louis Jourdan.*

Hitchcock extravaganza, where glamorous settings and eye-catching costumes were at least as important as the element of suspense. A fantasy about the life of the super-rich — stylishly tongue-in-cheek, sometimes witty — it might be considered a fore-runner of the all-conquering James Bond genre.

The story concerns a former cat-burglar, John Robie (Cary Grant), who has retired to spend his ill-gotten gains on the French Riviera. He is outraged when a number of burglaries are committed in the leading hotels, because although all the robberies bear his hallmark, he has had nothing to do with them. Purely for his own self-respect, the thief sets out to catch a thief, and the fun begins.

A rich American matriarch, Mrs Stevens (Jessie Royce Landis), is staying in the same hotel, husband-hunting for her beautiful frigid daughter Frances (Grace). Frances is attracted to Robie, but suspects he may be the thief. When her mother's jewels are added to the cat-burglar's spoils, Frances joins forces with Robie to track down the slippery criminal: after an exciting chase over the rooftops, they corner the miscreant, who turns out to be the daughter of Robie's old partner-in-crime.

The result was a feast for the eye, if not for the brain. One of the most spectacular (and now of course horrifyingly ironic) sequences showed Frances (Grace) driving a terrified Robie at a reckless pace round the twists and turns of the Moyenne Corniche, and there was another strong dose of local colour when police gave chase in the famous flower market. The critics were split. *Variety* called it "disappointing"; the *Los Angeles Times* praised it as "a high-polish job, a kind of reversion to the urbanities of a gentleman Raffles, with Cary Grant and Grace Kelly ideal in the romantic leads", while the London *Daily Telegraph* was cautiously approving: "The mood throughout is one of cynical humour, with witty dialogue and amorous over-tones. The young American beauty pursues the former jewel-thief with a Shavian frankness and zest, and their love scenes will entertain many people not ordinarily over-fond of thrillers. Mr. Grant and Miss Kelly dominate the film with easy charm. . ." Predictably perhaps the film was selected for Britain's Royal Film Performance.

Everyone involved with *To Catch a Thief* agreed that it was a pleasure to make. Director and stars knew each other well and worked together in exceptional harmony; Hitchcock kept to a strict but reasonable schedule and allowed his actors plenty of time for relaxing and sight-seeing.

Nevertheless, by the time she reached the Riviera for the location shots, Grace was near the end of her tether. She had been working intensively for five years and made nine films; even for one of her exceptional stamina, breaking-point was not far away. Even though she responded with her usual zest to Hitchcock's direction, and conscientiously put everything she could into her role, it would have been strange if, subconsciously at least, she had not begun to hanker for a change.

Her battles with Hollywood had increased her natural capacity for keeping her thoughts to herself, and no hint of any plans to change her life-style showed when she returned to California in the summer of 1955.

During her visit to Cannes MGM had been busy considering new options for her, but she still refused to be swayed by the lure of big names or exotic locations. During the next few months a number of announcements about her were made and subsequently retracted by the studio: she was to play in Tennessee Williams's *Cat on a Hot Tin Roof* (the part which eventually went to Elizabeth Taylor); she would do a musical called *The Opposite Sex*; she would star as the poet Elizabeth Barrett Browning in *The Barretts of Wimpole Street*, and opposite Stewart Granger in *Designing Woman*. All these plans fell through.

As the summer of 1955 turned to autumn, she began work on the movie version of *The Swan* (1956) as Princess Alexandra, a role she had already played on television. In this dreamy, graceful fantasy of Ruritanian life, the Princess, whose family fortunes are in decline, is persuaded to captivate the rich Prince Albert (Alec Guinness) to save her father's kingdom from ruin. A handsome tutor (Louis Jourdan) is hired to teach her the regal arts she will need as Albert's bride, and the whole plan nearly founders when she falls in love with him. Duty prevails, however: holding her head high "like a white swan," Alexandra marries her prince.

The film was a frothy, over-sweet concoction in which Grace was required to do little more than fence and dance elegantly, casting wistful glances at the handsome mentor. She did it beautifully, and also learned to ride side-saddle, which became her favourite way of riding thereafter.

Nobody except Grace herself had any inkling of how curiously prophetic *The Swan* would prove to be. But the remarkable fact was that within six months she became a real princess, landed with the task of helping revive a run-down Ruritanian principality. Oscar Wilde — could he have witnessed it — would surely have been delighted by this perfect example of nature imitating art.

On December 23rd 1955 Grace finished work on the film and flew home to Philadelphia for a traditional Kelly clan Christmas. As a rule this was an intimate occasion for members of the family only. . . but this year an unexpected guest had been invited.

Learning to fence with Louis Jourdan, Grace registers a hit in The Swan.

Finally reconciled to marriage with her Prince: Grace and Alec Guinness in The Swan.

4

THE WORLD AT HER FEET

hen Grace Kelly became engaged in 1956, her mother claimed — perhaps in a state of euphoria — that Prince Rainier was at least the fiftieth man who had proposed to her. If her daughter had added one charm to her bracelet for every suitor rejected, she said, she would by then have hardly been able to lift her wrist.

It was scarcely surprising that someone so beautiful should always have attracted boyfriends or that her mother should have made every effort to protect her from anyone she thought unworthy of such a prize. According to Mrs. Kelly, the first serious proposal came from a boy called Walter when Grace was still in her teens. Luckily, perhaps, Walter was pinned down by Navy service, and though he wrote several letters begging Grace to wait for his release, she had grown out of him by the time he became available.

Her next affair was much more traumatic. A school dance was planned for Christmas Eve and Harper Davis, a close friend of Grace's brother Kell, was short of a partner. Together with Kell he approached Mrs. Kelly to ask if he might invite Grace. After some hesitation Mrs. Kelly agreed — and so gave the go-ahead to a relationship which affected her daughter deeply.

Grace went off to the dance in her first long dress, and her mother, full of anxiety, waited up to see her safely home. Thereafter Harper took Grace out many times; to dances, sports events and films —

Pictures on the wall: Grace at the height of her Hollywood fame surveys some of the evidence of past successes.

but none of the family realised how much he meant to her until he fell ill with multiple sclerosis.

At first, when he was in bed at home, Grace would go to see him and return in tears. Later he was put into hospital, and everyone had to face the awful truth that he would never recover; friends and neighbours collected money to buy him a television set, to which Grace contributed. She visited him to the end, and even when he was paralysed and speechless, she mastered her grief with extraordinary self-control.

Ten years later, when her engagement was announced, and a reporter asked her if she had ever been in love before, she replied, in a careful voice: "Yes. I was in love with my first boy friend. His name was Harper Davis, and he died."

As she started to become famous in Hollywood, the gossip-writers, frustrated by her obvious integrity, maliciously invented romantic connections with any attractive man she met in public or in private. Just as journalists jumped to pair her off with Clark Gable when she went to Africa, so they fastened on her association with Ray Milland with whom she worked on *Dial M for Murder*.

It so happened that soon after the film was finished Milland and his wife announced that they were going to separate. The Press reaction was instant and inevitable: Milland was leaving his wife to marry Grace Kelly. Quite by chance Mrs. Kelly was on her way to the West Coast of America to spend some time with her daughter, and her arrival in Hollywood threw gallons of fuel on the flames: obviously, she had come to put an end to the affair between Grace and Ray Milland. The stories were all nonsense: if any attachment had begun, Grace herself had put an end to it long ago.

Next in line for speculation was Bing Crosby, with whom she made *The Country Girl* in 1953. Because Bing was a widower, and supposedly in search of a new wife, he had only to be seen taking Grace out for rumours to start, and the fact that she played his wife in the film made speculation still more rife. It was the same with William Holden, with whom the film had her fall in love: once spotted holding her hand, he too hit the headlines.

No-one persecuted Grace more savagely than the columnist Hedda Hopper, who seemed to have conceived a virulent hatred for her and warned other producers and directors not to use her, on the grounds that she was a nymphomaniac. Though manifestly absurd, these rumours wounded Grace deeply, and she came to loathe Hollywood, which she later described as a ''town without pity.''

''Only success counts,'' Grace said. ''Anyone who doesn't have the key which opens the door is treated like a leper. I know of no other place in the world where so many people suffer from nervous breakdowns, where there are so many alcoholics, neurotics and so much unhappiness.''

A suitor more sinister than any actor, from the family's point of view, was the smooth and internationally-mobile dress-designer Oleg Cassini. Born in Paris, of Russian descent, and thoroughly cosmopolitan, Cassini first set up business in Rome, but then moved to New York and quickly went through two wives; first the heiress Merry Fahrney, then the actress Gene Tierney, by whom he had two daughters. This alone did nothing to endear him to the Kelly family, and, even though he was an excellent tennis player and had represented Italy in the Davis Cup, with typical Kelly robustness they considered his profession effeminate.

Having met Grace in New York, he pursued her with truly Gallic verve and tenacity. So infatuated did he become that one evening, when she positively invited him to come and date her, he rushed out of his house in a state of high excitement, and dived into the swimming pool; only to find, too late, that there was no water in it! He survived.

When Grace came to France to make *To Catch a Thief* on the Riviera, he followed her to Cannes, stayed in the same hotel, took her out to dinner every night after shooting finished, and generally looked after her in the most affectionate way. His four-month campaign almost succeeded: in spite of the obvious difficulties, he persuaded her to become unofficially engaged.

To keep their liaison from the press, they travelled back to America separately — she by boat, he by air. The ruse was not very successful, for in September it was reported that Hollywood expected them to an-

nounce their engagement any day. ''With such a husband,'' commented one exceptionally banal columnist, ''Grace Kelly would become one of America's best-dressed women.''

Considerations of this kind cut no ice with Mrs. Kelly, and nor could Grace herself break through her mother's opposition. Perhaps in the heady, exotic atmosphere of the Riviera she had been over-optimistic about her chances of winning parental assent; now she met a brick wall of disapproval, and her mother did not mind making it clear to the press that it was she who gave the affair its *coup de grace*. ''I put it to him bluntly one afternoon in New York,'' she said. '' 'Look here, Oleg,' I told him. 'You're a charming escort, but in my opinion you're a very poor risk for marriage.' '' This head-on attack apparently unsettled both partners, and the protracted wrangling which ensued led to one memorable exchange of pleasantries. When Hedda Hopper wrote that she could not imagine what

Dogs were an important element in Grace's life. This Weimaraner puppy, given to her just before she sailed for Europe in 1956, accompanied her to Monaco on the liner.

Stars meet at New York International Airport, September 1964: Grace, on vacation from Hollywood with Elizabeth Taylor en route to England, and Lorraine Day, bound for a baseball match.

Pause for reflection: a cup of coffee and a hair-do while making Rear Window *in 1953.*

"She was born to be a princess," said Frank Sinatra, who starred with her so memorably in High Society.

Cheek-to-cheek with the Oscar statuette: Grace with her Academy Award as Best Actress of 1954 for her role as Georgie Elgin in The Country Girl.

Grace saw in Cassini, unless it was his moustache, he cabled back the immortal reply: "I'll shave mine if you shave yours."

Both before and after her involvement with Cassini, Grace was a close friend of Jean Pierre Aumont, a widowed French actor nearly twenty years her senior. Although their relationship lasted nearly two years, it seemed to accelerate suddenly at the time of the Cannes Film Festival in 1955. Meeting for lunch at a supposedly secret rendez-vous, the couple did not realise that a hidden cameraman with a telephoto lens was recording the scene for posterity. His pictures, published in *Life* magazine, showing them holding hands, kissing, and clearly on the closest of terms, caused uproar on both sides of the Atlantic. Never before had anyone managed to break into Grace's private life so effectively.

A few days later English papers reported that Aumont had announced their engagement. "I adore her," he is supposed to have said. "She's wonderful. She's charming, adorable, intelligent, and, in spite of her beauty, modest."

Most people agreed wholeheartedly with this assessment. But whether Aumont ever did announce their engagement, or whether he was merely reported to have done so, remains a matter of doubt. In any case, there was no positive follow-up.

The couple vanished temporarily, and the papers launched into a frenzy of speculation. When Grace failed to check in at her hotel in Paris, it was reported that she and Aumont had eloped. Next morning she reappeared but immediately departed for an unknown destination. When eventually cornered, she gave evasive replies. But then, both in Paris and New York, she emphatically denied that she was about to get married. "I have no plans for marriage at the moment," she said. "Talk of marriage is premature."

As far as Aumont was concerned, she was no doubt telling the truth. But she may already have had, at the back of her mind, another possibility about which nobody else yet knew.

It was during that controversial Cannes Festival of 1955, at which she was photographed with Aumont, that she first met His Serene Highness Prince Rainier III of Monaco. It seems ironic that the meeting which changed her life was set up simply as a publicity stunt. No disingenuous matrimonial designs motivated Pierre Galante, an editor of *Paris Match* and the husband of Olivia de Havilland, when he asked Grace if she would go to Monaco and meet its ruler during the festival: all he wanted was a good story for his magazine. Rainier, for his part, enjoyed meeting glamorous film-stars, and welcomed any publicity which might attract money-spending tourists to Monaco.

After a breakneck drive from Cannes, during which the car carrying the *Paris Match* photographers rammed the back of the one in which Grace was riding, she arrived at the Palace in a great rush, to find that Rainier was not yet back from lunch. As the minutes passed, and he still did not return, she almost gave up. Then, as she was on the point of leaving, he arrived: when they met, she offered her hand, and the Prince bowed. A few minutes later he was conducting her on a personal tour of the Palace and its grounds. The photographers took volleys of pictures inside the Palace and out, and Galante's day was made.

As befitted a fine actress, the film star gave no hint that the meeting had meant anything special to her. As she was swept back to the exigent demands of the Cannes Festival, she made no mention of the Prince to anyone. Not until months later did she reveal that she had been bowled over by Rainier's direct

A new role to learn: Grace with His Serene Highness, Prince Rainier III of Monaco, after the announcement of their engagement on January 6th, 1956.

simplicity. In Monaco, however, her visit caused an immediate stir. According to Father Francis Tucker, Rainier's private chaplain and confidant, for the next few days the Palace was "all aglow". The Prince, he said, took every possible opportunity of mentioning Grace: he was full of "little exuberances", and showed unusual interest whenever he read a news item about Grace.

Over the next few months the puckish Father Tucker (a Franciscan Friar) achieved a certain notoriety with his claims that it was he who engineered the great match. Certainly he wrote Grace an unctuous letter saying what a deep impression she had made, and clearly he tried to encourage her. Yet the man who really forged the link between Monaco and Philadelphia was Russ Austin, an old friend of Grace's father.

Arriving in Monte Carlo during the summer, and being told that no table was available at the Casino, Austin put a telephone call straight through to the Palace and explained who he was to Father Tucker. The priest passed on the message to Rainier, with the result that Austin not only got a well-placed table at the Casino, but found himself invited to the Palace next day.

There, taking his leave of the Prince, he issued a cheerful open invitation. If ever Rainier was in America, he said, he must be sure to look the Austins up.

At the time the Prince disclaimed any plans for crossing the Atlantic. Nevertheless, in mid-December that year he arrived in New York with Father Tucker and his personal physician, ostensibly for a medical check-up. At once he made contact with the Austins, and they, sensing what was in the air, contrived a special arrangement: instead of inviting the royal party to their own home, they arranged for Grace's mother to invite both themselves and the travellers to the Kelly household. There a party ensued: though tense at first, Grace soon settled into a merry conversation with Rainier, and everyone could see that a special rapport was quickly developing between them. Within two days over Christmas the Prince had asked her to marry him, and she had agreed.

Although no official announcement was made at the time, enough rumours of what was happening leaked out to frustrate a grotesque plot which was

Serene amidst the chaos of film-making, Grace on the set of High Society *in 1956. Already Prince Rainier had announced that this was the last film she would make.*

The girl in white gloves gets her man: Grace poses with Rainier at the party given in the Waldorf Astoria Hotel, New York, to celebrate their engagement.

then being hatched in New York. For months it had been apparent that Rainier's search for a wife was growing more and more urgent. Simultaneously, the Greek shipping millionaire Aristotle Onassis had invested a vast amount of money in Monaco, and wanted new attractions which would increase the influx of tourists. His friend George Schlee therefore consulted Gardner Cowles, publisher of *Look* magazine, about what they could do. Cowles came up with a novel idea: that they should float Marilyn Monroe across Prince Rainier's nose, like a fly over a salmon, and see if he would snap her up as his wife. Marilyn in Monaco, they thought, would be an irresistible lure to American tourists; a princess with her colouring and vital statistics would pull them in like nothing else on earth.

According to Cowles, he actually outlined the idea to Marilyn, who agreed to give it a try. Luckily the scheme died in infancy. But even the shock-

hardened readers of the *Journal American* were scandalised when the gossip columnist Dorothy Kilgallen revealed some similar plot, or a version of this one, claiming that "a man who knows the Prince" had approached her at a party given by the composer Richard Rodgers and "offered to split the 'dowry commission', or whatever Europeans call commission on an arranged marriage," if she would introduce Rainier to Marilyn.

All such schemes were overtaken by reality when the engagement was made public on January 5th 1956. The Prince's family's plan was that simultaneous announcements should be made in Monaco and Philadelphia, but because, in their excitement, they forgot about the five-hour time difference between Europe and America, the news broke first in Monaco and winged its way across the Atlantic, rather spoiling the impact of the Press conference called in the Kellys' home. In fact Mrs. Kelly had given the game away the night before when, in an unguarded moment, she had said, "Here I am, a bricklayer's wife, and now my daughter's going to marry a prince."

No matter: Mr. and Mrs. J.B. Kelly declared themselves happy to announce the betrothal of their daughter Grace to His Serene Highness Prince Rainier III of Monaco. Grace, who wore a dress of gold brocade and sat on a sofa holding her fiancé's arm, said that she did not know, or mind, whether the ceremony would be held in America or in Monaco, but that she expected to live in Monaco once she was married. When asked if she intended to go on with her screen career, she avoided any direct answer; all she would say was that under the terms of her contract with MGM she still had two films to complete.

In Monaco the announcement was said to have provoked "a lively enthusiasm", and the whole principality came out in a rash of celebratory red and white flags.

In due course it was decided that the wedding would be in Monaco, and that its date would be April 18th. Before then, however, Grace had one major professional obligation to discharge, and it could hardly have been more appropriate. She had agreed to take the role of the society beauty, first played by Katherine Hepburn, in a remake of *The Philadelphia Story*, now to be titled *High Society* (1957).

The film was to be produced by Sol C. Siegel, with songs by Cole Porter, and Grace's co-stars were Bing Crosby, Frank Sinatra, and Celeste Holm — not forgetting the inimitable Satchmo, Louis Armstrong, playing himself, and his Band. The scenario had been switched from the territory of Philadelphia's blue-bloods to Newport, Rhode Island, principally to give prominence to the

Newport Jazz Festival which C.K. Dexter-Haven (Crosby), ex-husband of lovely iceberg Tracy Lord (Grace), is helping to organise. Though divorced, Tracy and Dexter still live in neighbouring houses, and he still loves her. She, however, has found another man, the worthy, rich, square George Kittredge (John Lund) and is about to marry him.

When a brace of reporters (Sinatra and Holm) are sent to cover the society wedding against Tracy's wishes, she sets out to baffle and confuse them in a variety of ways which culminate with her drinking too much at her eve-of-wedding party, and plunging fully dressed into the swimming pool. After some straight talking all round, she throws Kittredge over in favour of remarriage with Dexter-Haven.

It was a glorious, glamorous romp: although Grace was new to musicals, her duet with Crosby, ''True Love'', was a highly polished piece of harmonising, which she sang herself in a clear, attractive voice. Above all, the film showed what her close friends had always known, that the 'fair Miss Frigidaire' was a brilliant mimic and comedienne with a superb sense of timing. For the first time in a film she allowed her sense of fun to sparkle: her performance had the fizz of the very best champagne. The scene in which she gave the interloping reporters The Treatment, fluttering round them like a ballet-mad butterfly, chattering feverishly in both French and English, interrupting their bemused replies and twisting every word they uttered, had a diamond-like brilliance, and her look of mischief as she decided how to deal with them revealed a whole side of her personality never before shown on celluloid.

It was as if her engagement, and the decisions she had taken about her future, had freed her from former inhibitions. In *High Society* she let herself go as never before. Another strange feature of the film was the way in which the script echoed reality: just as *The Swan* had seemed to forecast her own future, her real life. In the film Tracy Lord's mother told her that she had a fine body and a fine mind, and should not waste them on inferior men; and the picture's heroine, just like the actress who played her, was plagued by the constant harassment of ''arrogant reporters''.

Prince Rainier and his father, the Duke of Polignac, visited the set of *High Society*; however a lunch laid on for them was a disaster. Belittling remarks were made about the size of Rainier's principality, and Celeste Holm later claimed that she was sure, even then, that Grace would never return to film-making.

In a sense, Hollywood had done her proud. Her short career had spanned only five years; in that brief time she had made eleven films and starred

''It was as if her engagement, and the decisions she had taken, had freed her from former inhibitions. In High Society *she let herself go as never before.''*

with the leading actors of the day. Yet only her own good sense and the inspired direction of Hitchcock, Seaton, and, early on, John Ford, had saved her from being totally miscast and forced into a mould she could not and would not fit. MGM never understood her: she was beyond them. Without her own ironclad determination to do nothing cheap or untrue to herself, her career might just have fizzled out.

During her last few weeks in America she was under tremendous strain. Fully engaged as she was by her film work, she had at the same time to prepare, physically and emotionally, for a huge step into the unknown. Her life was made no easier by the continuous harassment of reporters.

As April 1956 approached she had to devote more and more time to fittings for her trousseau, and her final ten days on American soil melted away in a whirl of last-minute preparation and packing. Her trousseau was said to have cost the equivalent of £15,000, all of which she paid herself, from her enormous film earnings. The most expensive item was a £4,500 full-length Canadian sable coat, the next most exotic a full-length leopard-skin coat and a £3,000 mink jacket. Besides these the trousseau included six cocktail dresses, four summer dresses, two evening dresses, two ball gowns, several light coats

and a dozen hats. Everything had been designed in the United States — a 100 per cent American wardrobe for a 100 per cent American girl. The one garment whose details were kept secret was the wedding dress, which was sent to Europe aboard the liner *Constitution* incognito in a long steel box. When pressed for details about it, its designer gave away nothing except for the safe assertion that it would become ''the most-copied wedding dress in history.''

Grace's departure for Europe on April 4th, a rainy, windswept morning, took place amid scenes of hysterical excitement. Wearing a smart, single-breasted beige tweed suit, but no jewellery of any kind, she was driven to the docks in an anonymous black car.

No sooner was she on board than she made her first broadcast to her future subjects, a link-up having been specially arranged between Radio Monte Carlo and the Voice of America. After a rather trite opening, she hit a warm and touching note:

Afloat on her High Society *honeymoon — which, prophetically, took place on a yacht — Tracy Lord (Grace) planted a kiss on the lips of her husband C.K. Dexter-Haven (Bing Crosby).*

''I would like to tell my future compatriots that the Prince, my fiancé, has taught me to love them. I feel I already know them well, thanks to what the Prince has told me, and my dearest wish today is to find a small place in their hearts. . .''

The broadcast finished, she faced her final ordeal in America — a packed and frantic Press conference in the ship's observation lounge, where about 200 reporters and photographers struggled to secure her attention. Such was the scramble to get near her that officials became alarmed and began to shout, ''Give the lady air, please! Come on, now!'' Throughout the chaos Grace herself seemed unmoved, and when the horde had been driven back she answered questions with immaculate diplomacy:

Would you like a large family?

I hope I have one — yes.

How do you feel about leaving the United States?

I hope I shall be coming back to America quite often. I have a deep affection for my country. I hope to be back here on a visit with the Prince in the fall.

How do you feel about getting married?

Like any girl feels — very happy and very excited.

Will you continue your screen career?

Right now I'm too interested in my marriage career to think of the movies.

What do you call the Prince?

I call him Rainier.

What about a pet name for him?

That's between us.

How about your citizenship in future?

On my marriage I shall become a Monegasque, but it will not affect my American citizenship. I shall have dual citizenship.

Will your children be American citizens?

I don't know, but I doubt it.

Is any dowry involved in the marriage?

No. But I'm taking a present to the Prince. I can't tell you what it is, because I want it to be a surprise, like his to me.

One major surprise which she did spring on the Press corps was the fact that she had not spoken to her fiancé since his departure for home three weeks before. They had kept in touch, she said, by writing to each other every second day.

Several members of the Kelly family were unable to go with her, among them her sister Lizanne and her brother Jack's wife Mary, both of whom were expecting babies. Even so, the party consisted of about eighty people, and Grace alone had sixty pieces of baggage, to say nothing of her poodle Oliver and a Weimaraner puppy.

The eight-day voyage from the New World to the Old offered her little respite from the attentions of the newshawks; many of the leading magazines and newspapers in America and France had booked representatives on board the *Constitution*. But she treated them all with the unfailing courtesy for which she was already renowned.

Meanwhile, in Monaco, her fiancé had become noticeably irritable. He had been making all the arrangements for the wedding himself, and was obviously worn out. Then it became known that he had been suffering from toothache. When it was reported that he had had a tooth taken out, everyone hoped that his temper would improve. On the night of April 8th, with the *Constitution* in mid-ocean, he threw a stag party at an *auberge* up in the French mountains. The fact that Father Tucker received no invitation was interpreted as a sign of displeasure on the Prince's part: the priest, it was said, had dis-

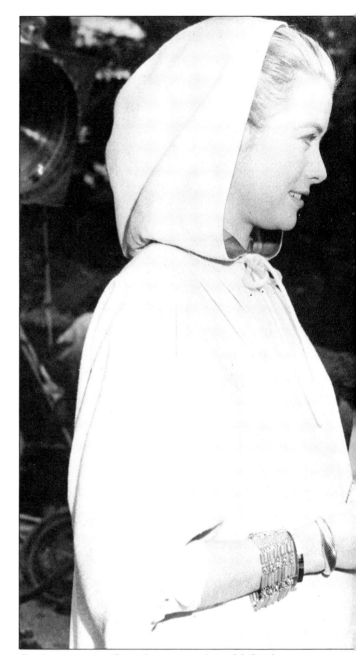

Satchmo says. . . Grace in conversation with Louis Armstrong at Bel-Air, San Francisco, in January 1956 during the filming of High Society.

Monaco-bound, the crew of the liner CONSTITUTION parade on deck as the ship prepares to leave New York, bearing Grace and her party, 80-strong, to her wedding: April 4th, 1956.

closed too many details of the courtship.

Anticipation in the principality had been steadily rising, and it reached fever pitch by the time the *Constitution* sailed into the Bay of Hercules off Monaco at 9.45 on the morning of April 12th. The day was gloomy and overcast, but the harbour breakwaters, the Casino terraces and the ramparts of the old town were already packed by a crowd of some 20,000 people.

Prince Rainier, who had been aboard his yacht *Deo Juvante II* since 6.30 am, immediately sailed out to meet his bride. As he went out of the harbour, smiling and waving from the bridge, people on the breakwater noticed that he had lost a lot of weight in the past few weeks. He looked slim, relaxed, and much younger than his photographs suggested.

As the yacht came out into the bay, a shoal of smaller boats, laden to the gunwales with journalists and cameramen, swarmed into position all round it. Gently the *Deo Juvante II* eased alongside the *Constitution* — a minnow in the lee of a whale — and a gang-plank was lowered on to the yacht's bridge. Down it came Grace, with her poodle in her arms. She wore a navy-blue waisted coat over a matching dress, with white gloves, a white flowered corsage and a pearl necklace. But the most striking feature of

Grace (banjo) compares notes with James Stewart (trombone). Their partnership in Rear Window *(1954) confirmed her status as a star.*

A star-studded cast. To include Louis Armstrong and the Newport Jazz Festival, the story's setting was changed from Philadelphia to Newport, Rhode Island.

As Grace crossed the Atlantic on her way to Monaco, her fiancé bombarded her with telegrams.

her outfit was a huge white hat which, to the great rage and disappointment of the onlookers, completely obscured her face. Only when she occasionally glanced upwards could people see her dazzling smile.

She and the Prince greeted each other rather formally: a strong, tight hand-clasp, but no embrace or kiss. Then he welcomed her parents and took them all into the saloon.

The yacht turned for the harbour, and as it came in past the breakwater a tremendous welcome erupted. The crowds burst into cheers. The yachts in the basin blasted off with their sirens. Artillery boomed out a salute, and a passing train added hoots to the joyous cacophony. Overhead a helicopter circled and a seaplane belonging to Aristotle Onassis let fall a fantastic rain of red-and-white flowers, while rockets climbed past them into the sky.

As soon as the yacht docked, officials of the principality came on board for a champagne reception, which was enlivened by an outburst of snapping and barking as Grace's two dogs had a difference of opinion. Then the Prince handed her onto the gangway, and as she walked ashore amid renewed

The big moment for the people of Monaco as their Princess-to-be came ashore with her fiancé from his yacht DEO JUVANTE II. But they did not like her hat which prevented them from seeing her face!

At the Wedding Eve Serenade, 400 singers, dancers and musicians, assembled in the square, entertained the bridal couple, who listened from a balcony of the Palace.

cheering, the sun providentially burst through the clouds, bathing her in a sudden blaze of light.

The landing ceremony seemed all too short. A smile to the crowd, a wave, and she was being whisked away in a bright-green car which drove her to the Palace. There in the cobbled courtyard a guard of honour, resplendent in red-feathered helmets, snapped to attention, and she entered her future home to the cry of bugles. Later she gave people a better chance to judge her beauty when she and Rainier came out onto the balcony and waved to the crowds below. If her gestures acknowledging the cheers were more careful than easy, there was no restraint about the wonderful smile with which she turned to the Prince before they went back indoors.

Hollywood itself could hardly have devised a more spectacular welcome. In the bars of Monaco that evening much grumbling was heard about the proportions of the all-obliterating hat: though people liked what they had seen, they had not seen enough. They can hardly be blamed for failing to realise what a priceless jewel the principality had landed.

5

THE GRIMALDIS OF MONACO

What sort of a man, then, was the Prince who had won Grace's hitherto inaccessible heart? And what was the miniature state which she was going to share?

Monaco is a rocky headland on the Mediterranean coast of France, and the whole territory of the principality (less than 500 acres) can be overlooked from the terrace of the sixteenth-century Royal Palace. But although it is so small, the state has a long and proud history.

The place was known to early navigators from Byblos, Tyre, and Sidon. These Phoenicians brought silk and oils and precious spices to trade with the local inhabitants: they also brought their god, a strange legendary figure called Melkart, known to the Romans as Hercules Monoikos — Hercules who dwells alone. So the Romans called the bay Portus Hercules Moneici, and in 122 AD the Roman domination of Provence began.

In the Middle Ages the Genoese built two castles on Monegasque territory; the first stones of the one on the cliff where the palace now stands were laid in 1215 (incidentally the year in which King John of England signed the Magna Carta).

Two factions were then struggling for supremacy on the Mediterranean coast: the Guelfs, who supported the Pope, and the Ghibellines, who were allies of the German Emperor. For the best part of a century they wrangled, and in 1295 open war broke

out when they slaughtered one another in the streets of Genoa.

The Grimaldi family, who were Guelfs, were exiled when the Ghibellines triumphed, but went on waging sporadic warfare against their rivals. In 1297 one of their number, François Grimaldi, known as *Malice,* dressed up as a monk and was admitted to the Genoese fortress in Monaco. Drawing a sword from beneath his monk's habit, he admitted his band of followers, and took the garrison by surprise. From that day to this — apart from two short breaks the territory has been ruled by the Grimaldis, and in remembrance of that exploit, two monks with drawn swords support the Grimaldi coat of arms.

The Grimaldis are therefore Europe's oldest ruling family. But although they have reigned for so long over their small principality, its history has been turbulent. Savoy and Milan, France and Spain have all cast covetous eyes over the flourishing trading-post, with its enviable climate and safe harbour. Nor were family relationships always harmonious. Although Lambert Grimaldi, who married the Monegasque heiress Claudine, managed the diplomatic balance between his powerful neighbours with great astuteness, quarrels broke out between his sons. In 1505 Lucien Grimaldi assassinated his tyrannical older brother Jean II, and the following year the Genoese, sensing weakness, moved in like sharks to the kill.

By December 1506 there were 14,000 Genoese soldiers besieging Monaco, and for four months the small defending force of 1,500 Monegasques, Provençals and Italians fought back from their rocky headland. In March 1507, they won the day. The invading force sailed away, and Lucien, who had

---

Pomp and ceremony in miniature: a procession leaves the 200-room Grimaldi Royal Palace in Monaco, with the Principality's national colours — red and white — much in evidence.

retrieved his reputation by his courage throughout the siege, began once more the diplomatic balancing-act between France and Spain which was necessary to preserve the integrity of his little domain. Although subject to the sovereignty of France, by the Treaties of Burgos and Tordesillas, Monaco came under the protection of the powerful Holy Roman Emperor, Charles V.

For 100 years the balancing act succeeded in keeping Monaco independent. Then in 1605 a Spanish garrison was installed, to the dismay of the Monegasques, and in 1612 the Ruler of Monaco, Honoré II, was compensated for this curtailment of his powers by Spain's recognition of his title as Serene Prince.

Not that this sop in any way lessened Honoré's determination to be his own master again. In November 1641 he put to flight the Spanish garrison with a well-timed attack, and restored the "Glorious liberty of Monaco", preferring to opt once-and-for-all for French, rather than Spanish protection.

To this day, Honoré II is a hero of Monegasque history: besides being a man of action, he was a patron of the arts who collected the works of Titian, Dürer, Raphael, Rubens and Michelangelo.

His successor, Louis I, codified the law which bears his name. A century later the tiny state was jolted from its provincial calm by the tumult of the French Revolution, and the great wave of anarchy that washed over its powerful neighbour spread ripples through Monaco as well. Reluctantly the Prince of the day, Honoré III, conceded reforms to his people, who had suddenly woken from contentment with their feudal system of government and joined in the intoxicating pipe-dream by which the French populace demanded Liberty, Equality, and Fraternity.

Peremptorily, the revolutionary generals called for the annexation of Monaco, confiscated the Prince's property and in 1793 imprisoned him in Paris. The following year he was released, but soon died far from home. His country remained in French hands for nearly twenty years until Napoleon, after his escape from Elba, met the future Prince Honoré V in Cannes shortly before the battle of Waterloo.

According to local legend, Napoleon asked the young prince where he was going, and Honoré replied: "Sire, you are returning to your states and I am going to govern mine."

The answer pleased the Emperor, who graciously allowed him to do as he wished.

After the Battle of Waterloo and Napoleon's downfall, the future of Monaco hung in the balance. By the Treaty of Vienna it was placed under the protection of the King of Sardinia, much to Monegasque annoyance; Sardinian troops were garrisoned in the town and there was further trouble from the cities of Menton and Roquebrune which clamoured for independence from Monaco.

Eventually the Sardinian troops were withdrawn when the Savoy family was granted the area round Nice. For an indemnity of four million francs Charles III gave up his right to Menton and Roquebrune, and took an important step in the development of Monaco when he agreed to allow the railway line from Genoa to Nice to pass through his territory. Monaco became a French Protectorate once more: it was about to enter a new era as one of the world's most popular tourist centres.

Charles III is regarded as Monaco's first truly modern prince, but credit for the enterprise which brought the rich and famous crowding into the tiny state should go to his mother, Princess Caroline, who suggested opening a gaming Casino.

In December 1856, a roulette wheel began to spin in the Palais de la Condamine, and although it was another twelve years before the opening of the railway made communications easy, the first determined gamblers were prepared to travel by horse-drawn coach over the precipitous mountain road past La Turbie and down the steep, winding descent to sea level for their sport.

A new Casino, with an elegant Palladian façade and chandeliers sparkling under the dome of its main hall, was finished in 1865. An astute financier, François Blanc, had bought out the original owners of the Casino for the then-enormous sum of two million francs. He held 22,000 of its 30,000 shares, and Charles III 400; together they set to work to make money from their new enterprise. The first priority was to create accommodation; the second to ensure a plentiful supply of visitors and also encourage more residents.

By building a new town, Monte Carlo, named after himself, Charles achieved his first objective, and when he abolished all rates and taxes in 1869 the population of his principality increased substantially. Splendid new hotels attracted the rich and famous of Northern Europe to spend their winters in the sun in Monaco, while the lure of the gaming tables ensured a healthy revenue.

Not that a gambler's life was entirely restful at that date. In the 1870s the captain of a Russian warship which had anchored in the bay at Monaco paid the casino a courtesy visit, and unfortunately gambled away all his ship's money. He went back on board, trained his guns on the casino, and threatened to blow it up if the money were not returned to him. The manager called for the French Navy, but no help was forthcoming. The first shell landed on the casino terrace; a white flag was run up, and the chief croupier put to sea with the required amount.

When Charles died in 1889, he bequeathed to his son Albert I a flourishing family enterprise. Prince Albert was a very different character from his astute and shrewd but somewhat melancholy father. He was a lively, action-loving young man with a passionate interest in marine biology and the new science of oceanography. Indeed it was his charts of the Mediterranean which were used by the Allies for their landings in the Second World War. He founded the majestic Oceanographic Museum on the Rock of Monaco which, with its huge collection of marine animals and large scientific library, is now one of the country's most fascinating buildings.

But Albert's preoccupation with scientific research may have contributed to his unsatisfactory domestic life. At the age of twenty-one, in 1869, he was pressed by his "protector", Napoleon III, to marry an English wife, and with some reluctance he chose the equally-reluctant Lady Mary Douglas-Hamilton, then aged eighteen. The marriage lasted less than a year. Trouble over the Princess's inheritance led to her being kept a virtual prisoner in the Palace. In a letter home she referred to "the bitterness of the weeks I spent in Monaco," and in 1870 she succeeded in escaping; she left for a cure in Baden-Baden, never to return.

A few months later she gave birth to a son, Prince Louis, and a long lawsuit ensued since she resolutely refused to go back to her husband. After an eight-year wrangle, the marriage was nullified by the Holy See, and Prince Albert was free to look for another bride.

By a strangely prophetic chance, the girl who won his heart was an attractive, intelligent, blonde American, who had been briefly married to the Duc de Richelieu. Like her successor nearly 70 years later, Alice Heine was the daughter of a self-made millionaire, and became a generous patron of the arts which, for the first time, began to influence the life of her adopted country. However, the durability of their marriages differed; in 1902 the marriage of Prince Albert and Princess Alice was dissolved and he returned to his lonely life of scientific research. In 1911 he accepted an enormous change in the constitution when he agreed to the election of a National Assembly of 18 members.

Throughout the First World War Monaco remained neutral; but the carefree epoch which had brought it such prosperity was swept away in the bloody maelstrom.

In 1922 Prince Albert died, leaving his throne to the child of his brief marriage to Mary Douglas-Hamilton, Prince Louis II. The cosmopolitan upbringing of the new Prince may have given him his rather light-hearted approach to his new responsi-

The sword-wielding monks in the Grimaldi coat of arms commemorate the occasion on which one of Prince Rainier's ancestors disguised himself as a friar and so gained entrance to the Genoese fortress in Monaco. Hence the motto Deo Juvante — *"with God's help".*

Salutes are fired over the harbour at Monaco to announce royal events. The Grimaldis have held the Principality for more than 700 years — far longer than any other European ruling family.

bilities. Certainly he spent little time in his principality. During the winter months he would visit the Palace to entertain and be entertained by the fashionable, sun-loving foreigners who had now acquired the habit of spending their winters in Monte Carlo. For the rest of the year he moved from one country estate to another, renting grouse moors

in Scotland for the shooting season, and administered his state from afar, with the help of a travelling bureaucracy of secretaries and ministers.

Work on the Port of Monaco, which had been dragging on since 1901 was completed during his reign. The Monte Carlo car rally, which had started under Prince Albert, received a new impetus when the Grand Prix de Monaco, the exacting race with a thousand bends, was instituted by the Automobile Club of Monaco. Louis also caused a large tunnel to be excavated under the Rock of Monaco to ease traffic congestion. The little state ticked over, but only 1939, the big-time gamblers who contributed so much to Monaco's finances were a dying species. The need for new sources of money was growing urgent.

Prince Louis may or may not have married the pretty laundress Juliette Louvet who gave birth to his daughter Charlotte. Certainly no marriage was officially acknowledged. Nevertheless, after a Parisian upbringing, the girl was summoned to Monaco by her grandfather to be tutored as a Princess and named next in succession after her father.

Princess Charlotte married Count Pierre de Polignac, son of the Duc de Polignac, and had two children, Antoinette and Rainier, the present ruler of Monaco, who was born in 1923. But this marriage, like so many others in the Grimaldi history, did not last. When the children were ten and six years old respectively, their parents separated. Princess Charlotte renounced her right to the throne in favour of her son, and went back to live near Paris, leaving the boy's education in the hands of his father.

By all accounts, Prince Rainier's early childhood was unsettled. He was deprived of any firm rock of

In Monaco's national costume, Grace poses with Albert (left), Stephanie, Caroline and Rainier, in the square outside the Grimaldi Palace, in 1974.

family life and affection. At the age of eight he was despatched across the Channel to an English preparatory school, where he suffered inevitable torments of homesickness, exacerbated by the need to communicate in a foreign language. As he told his official biographer, Peter Hawkins:

"I suppose I enjoyed it, but like most little boys who go to prep school, I was caned. This shocked me in the fact that it was a physical punishment, but no more. The attitude of all English youngsters at that age is that being caned is more of an occasion to have a good laugh, and fun, so there was nothing dramatic about it."

Already he was learning to keep a typically British stiff upper lip, but a glimpse of the loneliness of the small boy can be seen in his recollection: "When you are twelve years old, you feel that the Channel is terribly wide. The plane services weren't so regular in those days, either."

Still, he endured his exile philosophically, and learned to fight with his fists. In the appropriately flamboyant language of an official guide to Monaco, the Prince was a boxing champion "and without too many compliments in the most democratic way in the world often knocked out his Anglo-Saxon adversaries."

Despite this useful skill, he seems to have felt his isolation even more deeply when he went on to Stowe, the English public school whose boys are known as Stoics, not without reason. He ran away and got as far as Buckingham before the police caught up with him and returned him to school, where his house-master, to his credit, welcomed him back with an enormous tea. All the same, it cannot have been a happy period, and it was a relief to the young Prince to complete his education in Switzerland at the college of Le Rosey at Rolle.

This pleasant period was cut short when the Germans began to bombard Lyons and for his own protection Rainier was called home. There he began to see at first hand the workings of government. The impression he had formed as a child from watching Prince Louis' peripatetic administration — that to rule Monaco was really quite simple — received a sharp jolt. The closer he got to the job, the more difficult he realised it was.

The question of completing his education now became pressing, and despite the fact that most of France was under German occupation, he was sent to Montpellier University, where he sat for his *baccalauréat*. He studied political science for a year in Paris, finding it increasingly difficult to accept the presence of first Italian, then German troops in Monaco. As the Germans began to retreat, they were replaced by Polish and Czechoslovakian conscripts; but eventually the local resistance fighters drove them out too.

Ugly incidents followed as the *Maquis* settled old scores with locals who had been unwise enough to collaborate with the Germans. Rainier was glad to leave home and volunteer for the French Army of Algeria, in which he served as plain Lieutenant Grimaldi.

During the next year and a half, he fought in Alsace and was awarded the Croix de Guerre; then, at the cessation of hostilities, he joined the economic section of the French Military mission in Berlin.

This relative freedom was brought to an abrupt end in April 1949, when Prince Louis, after a long illness, delegated his powers to his grandson. A few months later he died.

Thus, at the age of twenty-six, Prince Rainier succeeded him and was crowned in the white-stone Cathedral of St. Nicholas overlooking the harbour. Dark and handsome in the Mediterranean way, of medium height and stocky build, the young Prince had become one of Europe's most eligible bachelors; but he showed no immediate inclination to marry.

Other matters required his attention first: urgent matters such as the modernisation and diversification of his principality, and above all the discovery of new sources of revenue. The prosperous and fashionable little state, which his grandfather had inherited, now looked distinctly run-down. The elegant buildings needed repair; and the Palace itself was barely fit to live in. The roofs were in a dire state and whole place had a desolate, defeated air as if it knew that its days of glory were past.

Saddest of all was the way Monaco's once-glamorous image had been tarnished. Monte Carlo no longer attracted the *beau monde*; as a playground for the rich and famous it had been superseded by other fashionable resorts. In Somerset Maugham's celebrated phrase, it had become "a sunny place for shady people". Wealthy foreigners no longer won and lost fortunes at the gaming-tables: there was an urgent need to attract people with ordinary incomes, so that the country's finances no longer depended so heavily on profits from the Casino.

As one of Rainier's counsellors explained: "We were rather like one of those rocks in the Antarctic which has always been the undisputed domain of the royal penguins. Then one day the King Penguin notices that his flock is not so numerous nor so full of fight any more, and all around the rock the sea is boiling with ordinary penguins struggling to get a foothold. The question is, how many penguins do you allow ashore without getting pushed off the rock yourself. . . ?"

While Rainier strove to find an answer to this question, he continued a longstanding friendship with the beautiful, but divorced, French actress

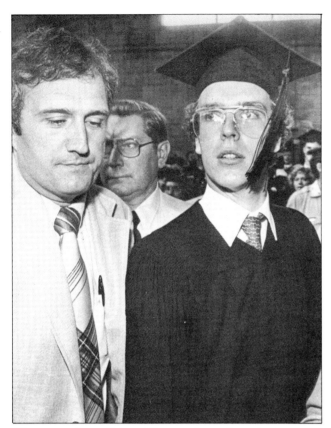

Heavy security as Prince Albert graduates from Amherst College, Massachusetts. Although younger than his sister Caroline, he became heir-apparent to the Principality of Monaco as soon as he was born.

Gisèle Pascal. His subjects watched and waited anxiously for signs of marriage. Human nature is sometimes deplorably selfish. The main source of their concern was not their Prince's happiness, but their own pockets. Under the 1918 agreement between France and Prince Albert, Monaco was recognised as an independent principality whose sovereignty could not be ceded to any foreign power except France. But if the throne of Monaco were ever to become vacant, France could immediately claim sovereignty over the whole principality.

The spectre of French taxes and French conscription descending on their sunny haven so alarmed the citizens of Monaco that their Prince's marriage and begetting of an heir became a serious matter. No-one took more interest in the subject than Aristotle Onassis, who had recently invested large sums of money in the archaically-named Société des Bains de Mer, which controlled the Casino. When Rainier set off for America and his momentous Christmas visit to Philadelphia in December 1955, his subjects awaited the outcome of his visit with barely controlled agitation.

The Prince was well aware of their preoccupation, but in six years of rule he had become adept at avoiding the gossip which is the breath of life to all small communities. While no-one expected him to marry Mlle. Pascal, his movements were closely monitored by his subjects, and, as he said himself, there were a whole lot of people who were "throwing up names" and thinking they could arrange his life: "My father kept telling me: 'Be careful, these people are trying to push their relatives in front of you'."

Whatever his position, Rainier himself was an attractive man with a robust sense of humour, a sportsman who had an unusual *rapport* with animals. Like the British Royal Family, he found great pleasure in the spontaneous affection of animals who neither knew nor cared that he was a Prince.

Early in his reign, in 1954, he created a Zoological Garden which is not, strictly speaking, a zoo but a "centre of acclimatisation" for different species of tropical animals, particularly from Africa. It is one of his favourite projects. The animals' spacious enclosures have views over the Mediterranean which many humans might envy, and while their creature comforts are supplied by a staff of experts, Rainier is careful not to neglect their mental well-being. Nowadays he often invites selected specimens to take holidays with him at his mountain farm. He is fearless in handling even the larger predators, and has said that if he were not a prince he would like to be a lion-tamer.

Though this ambition could hardly be fulfilled in the literal sense, metaphorically there were plenty of lions for him to subdue, but to do this successfully, he needed the help of a strong partner. Given his family's poor record in the domestic field, he longed for a marriage that would endure; a wife with whom he could share the burden of office and whose judgement he could trust.

When an importunate reporter asked him for a picture of the girl he would like to marry, the Prince patiently reeled off a list of attributes: it was extraordinary how accurately they described the girl from Philadelphia.

After his education at British schools he spoke English perfectly, with an authentic Oxford accent; an excellent raconteur, he had a predilection for risqué jokes. He had travelled about Europe enough to realise that Monaco's reputation hovered on the verge of absurdity — that many foreigners regarded his principality as no more than a running comic-opera performance in rather poor taste, where the brigandage of past centuries survived in the form of gambling and financial skulduggery.

And yet, though he could laugh at himself and his diminutive domain, he was serious and intelligent, and motivated by a strong sense not only of self-preservation, but also of duty towards his subjects.

6

A FAIRYTALE WEDDING

The Prince had made it known that he wanted "the richest ceremonial of the past" revived for his "beautiful wife", and his subjects were determined to see that he got it.

Nothing could have been more different from the simple ceremony in which Grace, as the Quaker bride, had been married in *High Noon*. For her real-life marriage to Prince Rainier of Monaco the entire principality was *en fête*. Three miles of red carpet were laid through the streets, open-air music-halls, balls, and cinemas were all free, champagne flowed everywhere, and every vase of flowers held a hidden Nikon or Hasselblad.

When they came ashore in Monaco Grace and her immediate family moved into a suite of rooms in the sixteenth-century Palace, while the Prince removed himself to his villa a few miles along the coast. Grace protested at such a Victorian arrangement, but her fiancé insisted that it should stand. The rest of the bride's party installed themselves in the Hermitage Hotel, and as guests began to flood in, celebration followed celebration.

Inevitably, with so many rich, famous and highly-strung people in close proximity to one another, there were occasional flare-ups of temperament. Those professional socialites Sir Bernard and Lady Docker, bringing a party of guests from their yacht

Regal splendour: Prince Rainier in full uniform with his bride in her wedding dress of ivory silk and Brussels lace. The Cathedral ceremony on April 19th, 1956, one of the first television spectaculars to be broadcast on Eurovision, was seen by about thirty million people.

Shemara to dine at the Cabaret Restaurant below the Casino, were furious to be refused admission. They had not been warned that the Kelly family had taken over the whole restaurant for the evening, and they retreated to *Shemara* to compose a stinging letter of protest to the Palace.

Photographers complained bitterly that rivals were being given better facilities, and some native Monegasques were alleged to have sold their invitations to Prince Rainier's garden party.

The Casino offered a spectacular gala in honour of the bridal couple in the Salon of the Winter Sporting Club, which had been transformed into a replica of the courtyard at Versailles. Facing the stage, in a box decorated in the inevitable red and white, Grace and Rainier watched Tamara Toumanova dance in a ballet; and Eddie Constantine, the American singer who had his greatest success in Paris, sang for them. The evening ended with a spectacular display of fireworks.

Wedding presents were carried into the Palace by the hundred. By the hand of her representative, Sir Guy Salisbury-Jones, Marshal of the Diplomatic Corps, Queen Elizabeth II sent an inscribed silver salver. The American and German colonies of Monaco presented a massive picture frame in solid gold and a delicate table-service of handworked porcelain, while the French President, M. Coty, gave a pair of decorated helmsman's wheels for the yacht, *Deo Juvante II*, which proved to be the Prince's present to his bride. (The French President's representative was M. François Mitterand.) A miniature revolving stage was given by the 44 members of the Festival Ballet Company. Passengers who had travelled with Grace on the *Con-*

stitution clubbed together to buy $14,000's worth of equipment for a cinema to be installed in the Palace. Three separate bridal "showers" organised by Grace's girlfriends in New York had already furnished her with the most glamorous store of underclothes that any feminine heart could have desired.

On the morning of April 18th the bride and groom, together with their witnesses, gathered in the throne room of the Palace for the civil wedding. Everyone appeared nervous and tense. Grace wore a rose-beige dress of Alençon lace on top of toning silk taffeta. Avoiding the mistake she had made on her arrival by wearing a huge hat, she had chosen instead a close-fitting Juliet cap. She took her place on one of the two red velvet chairs placed in front of the throne, on which the Princes of Monaco sit only on days of coronation.

A few feet away, Prince Rainier appeared thoroughly ill at ease. He was formally dressed in a black morning coat and grey striped trousers, and was obviously disturbed by the heat of the powerful television and cinema arc-lights, which had been placed far too close to him for comfort. He had given his bride a smile as he entered, but for the rest of the ceremony he stared straight ahead, occasionally biting the knuckle of his right index finger, a characteristic gesture of unease.

Besides the bride's parents, and the bridegroom's, there were also in the throne room the representatives of twenty-four nations, and the ceremony was conducted by M. Marcel Portanier, one of the senior Monaco judges. He seemed over-awed by his surroundings. After asking Rainier, as reigning prince, for permission to proceed, the judge continued: "The gravity of the declaration which I am about to hear, the nature of the consent which it is my task to receive, would be enough to justify my anxiety.

"But it is even more worrying for a magistrate who has never been confronted by such a gathering, by the impressive and intimidating presence in this historic place, the throne room, of the most eminent representatives of the great and numerous nations which have wished on this happy and moving occasion to demonstrate so brilliantly their vibrant sympathy for the Sovereign Prince of Monaco and his most gracious fiancée. . . "

Taking a deep breath, he went on to express the good wishes of all the Prince's loyal subjects and assure him that "a whole tiny nation is rejoicing today. This tiny nation is a big family, of which your Highness is the head."

At the end of his speech, the judge read out the civil code of Monaco which governs marriage. Articles 181, 182 and 183 assert that the married couple owe each other mutual fidelity and

Not quite at ease, Rainier and his bride pose after the civil wedding ceremony on April 18th, 1956. "Now I'm half-married," she said.

The Royal couple during the civil ceremony. Grace's dress was of rose-beige Alençon lace. Rainier was much harassed by the heat of the television lights.

In the Throne Room of the Royal Palace, Grace's family with her parents sitting in the centre, grit their teeth, as they endure the formalities of the civil marriage ceremony.

assistance. The husband must protect the wife, and the wife give her obedience to the husband. The wife is obliged to cohabit with the husband and follow him wherever he decides to live. The husband must receive the wife and supply her with all that she needs for her life, according to his means and position.

The long list of Rainier's titles followed, 142 in all. Finally, Grace Kelly, of far-off Philadelphia, by way of Hollywood, was asked if she would marry His Serene Highness Prince Rainier III of Monaco.

She replied, "Oui," in a quiet but clear voice.

The question was repeated, and Rainier also responded with an audible if low-pitched "Oui."

The heavy register was brought for the couple to sign; Prince Rainier first, and then his wife. Afterwards it was placed on a table to receive the signatures of the witnesses. At the close of the ceremony, representatives of the foreign nations, headed by the envoy from the Vatican, were presented to the Prince and his bride. Later, the couple made an appearance on the balcony in response to continuous cheering from the crowd gathered in the courtyard.

"Now I'm halfway married," said Grace; but she was to spend that night at the Palace, still as Miss Kelly, while Rainier returned to his villa on nearby Cap Ferrat once more.

After a week of unseasonable rain and humid, overcast skies, the sun suddenly shone brilliantly. All the guests were invited to lunch at the Palace, and the meal went on for so long that before it was finished the 3,000 Monegasques who had been invited to the afternoon garden party were already assembled and becoming restless. *Their* party finally began over half an hour late.

In the palm-shaded Palace garden, long tables were loaded with cake and champagne, and the red-and-white glasses from which the guests drank their loyal toasts were presented to them as souvenirs of the occasion. It was the first chance many Monegasques had been given to see their Prince's new American bride properly, and her beauty made a stunning impact on them. As one long-time resident exclaimed, "Her complexion is perfect, astonishing. . ."

Next in the festivities came a Gala at the Casino Opera. The London Festival Ballet Company performed a new work written for the occasion by Stan Kenton, with choreography by Michael Charnley, called *Homage to the Princess*, in which Belinda Wright and John Gilpin danced the principal roles. Grace, radiant in a diamond tiara and beaded dress with a full, bell-shaped skirt designed by Lanvin, wore Monaco's highest decoration, the Order of St. Charles, with which Prince Rainier had invested her

A fairy-tale bride, Grace arrives at the Cathedral on the arm of her father, John B. Kelly, in blazing sunshine, on the morning of April 18th, 1956.

after the civil ceremony, and also the diamond necklace which had been the gift of the people of Monaco.

The programme was diplomatically arranged to give equal prominence to the ballet troupe who had flown in from Paris. Other stars of the evening were Margot Fonteyn and Michael Soames, who danced an unforgettably romantic *pas de deux*.

If the couple in the red-and-white decked Royal Box felt the strain of the preceding days, they gave no sign of it. With the Kelly self-discipline, Grace smiled and waved to the cheering crowd as she and Rainier said a formal goodnight at the end of the evening and returned to their separate lodgings.

By now the whole Principality was en fête; the police were bombarded with complaints as pickpockets, pouring in from their other haunts on the Riviera, ran amok among the milling crowds!

A truce had at last been reached with the photographers whose behaviour had earlier threatened to ruin the dignity of the proceedings.

Grace found it difficult to slip the wedding ring on her finger, and had to enlist her bridegroom's help.

After one or two difficult confrontations, the Prince agreed to allow three representative press photographers into the throne room for pictures after the civil ceremony, and as the wet weather which had made the pressmen's job so disagreeable gave way to spring sunshine, tempers improved all round.

On April 19th 1956 the religious ceremony in the Cathedral of St. Nicholas provided a spectacle which no one present ever forgot. Television cameras gave an intimate view of the fairytale proceedings to an audience of thirty million people in nine countries, and although the bride and bridegroom resented this intrusion into their privacy, they strove heroically to conceal their feelings.

As Prince Rainier later told Peter Hawkins, his official biographer, ''There was such a lack of intimacy. . . For a man, perhaps, this is less important, but for the Princess it meant a great deal. It is difficult for a girl, for her wedding, if she can't be alone with herself for a moment. And the Princess did not have a minute to herself from the moment she set foot in the Principality.

''Another thing that astonished me when we actually stood together in the Cathedral was the fact that during this wedding in front of an altar there were cameras and microphones everywhere. Such lack of dignity and solitude. Reflecting on this afterwards, we both agreed that we should really have got married somewhere in a little chapel in the mountains. That is the sort of impossible desire one has after these things.''

Years later, Grace herself confirmed this verdict. When asked why they had both looked so strained during the service, she replied: ''It was partly seriousness about getting married, and partly the fact that there were 1,500 journalists in Monaco, most of them behind the altar or hanging from the rafters.''

It was indeed impossible to combine ''the richest ceremonial of the past'' with solitude and privacy. But for all the spectators, whether inside the Cathedral or watching on television, the sight of Princess Grace in her wedding dress was a dream come to life. The dress was the brainchild of Helen Rose, MGM's brilliant designer whose spectacular costumes Grace had worn in *The Swan* and *High Society*. The ivory gown and veil were made from 25 yards of *peau de soie,* 25 yards of silk taffeta, 100 yards of silk net and 300 of lace. The veil was sewn with myriad tiny pearls.

The fitted bodice had long, tight sleeves with scalloped wrists, and buttoned down from the high neckline to the waist. The skirt was very full, and its ten-foot train posed a problem for the bridesmaids when it caught on a chair. On her head the bride wore a petalled lace head-dress sewn with pearls above the shining coils of her chignon, which could be seen through the folds of the veil. In her ears were plain pearl studs. She looked like a fairytale bride, as people around the world have always recalled, when she emerged from the Palace on her father's arm and, followed by her procession of flower girls, pages and bridesmaids dressed in silk organza, crossed the cobbled courtyard to the Cathedral.

Prince Rainier was magnificently attired in a uniform of gold-striped blue trousers and gold-buttoned navy tunic, with gold-braided cuffs and epaulettes. Across his chest from right shoulder to waist was slung the red-and-white sash of the order of St. Charles, and the left side of his tunic blazed with decorations. A gold belt, shoulder cord and chain completed his regalia.

The ceremony, conducted by Monsignor Gilles Barthe, Bishop of Monaco, lasted nearly three hours, and was followed by a nuptial mass. Again, the couple were instructed in their obligations towards one another and asked if each took the other in marriage according to the rite of the Church. Again the Prince and his bride answered, ''Oui, je veux.'' (Yes, I will).

After the Mass, the representative from the Vatican delivered a personal message from the Pope. Then the newly-married couple processed down the aisle and out into the sunshine, where cheers and a salute of guns greeted them as they took their places in an open Rolls-Royce flying the Grimaldi standard. Off they drove on a tour of the Principality — stopping first at the shrine of a saint, where Grace left her bouquet — before returning to greet their 600 guests at the reception lunch.

The festivities continued — remarkably — with a visit to the National Stadium to watch a football game. Then, as the sun began to set over a magical domain, the Prince and Princess were driven once more to the harbour. There the white yacht, the 324 ton *Deo Juvante II*, awaited them, a haven of calm after the hectic turmoil of the past week.

They went aboard, waving to the thousands who had lined the harboursides and the hills above to wish them ''bon voyage''. A flotilla of small craft followed the yacht as she sailed majestically out into the bay; the ships in the harbour shrilled their sirens, and in the sky above the yacht hung two huge Grimaldi standards suspended by parachutes which had been fired aloft from the yacht belonging to Onassis.

Turning in the direction of Cap Ferrat, *Deo Juvante* disappeared from view.

The honeymoon was as relaxed and private a time as a honeymoon should be. Untroubled by the Press for the first time since the announcement of their engagement, Rainier and Grace recovered from the strain of the past weeks and enjoyed the simple pleasures of swimming, sunbathing and one another's company as *Deo Juvante II* made her leisurely way along the Mediterranean coast. Then they visited Spain, and sailed on to Corsica, where empty beaches of dazzling white sand offered perfect swimming and picnicking.

Princess Grace prays during the wedding service. But both she and Rainier were disturbed by the intrusive television cameras. ''There were 1,500 journalists in Monaco,'' she said later, ''most of them behind the altar or hanging from the rafters.''

Not even the most intimate moments of the service escaped the camera's eye. "Such a lack of intimacy," complained the Prince, "such a lack of dignity."

The ordeal of the Cathedral service over, the Princess comes down the great steps on her husband's arm. A fairy-tale had come true. But already people were asking: "Can it last?"

It must have been tempting to dream of sailing into the sunset and never returning to land. Aboard the yacht no one was watching to catch them out in some less-than-Royal gesture; there were no hidden cameras or microphones to forestall spontaneity or inhibit conversation. They could go ashore where they wished, when they wished, and escape back to their floating refuge as soon as they attracted unwelcome attention. As other royal honeymooners have recently found, there is no better way to begin your marriage than aboard your very own yacht.

An open Rolls-Royce gives citizens of Monaco the best possible view of their new Princess as she tours the streets of the Principality after the Cathedral service. By the time they returned to the palace, 600 guests had assembled for lunch.

7

PRINCESS GRACE

Just as the conspirators in the Marilyn Monroe plot predicted, the marriage had a startling effect on tourism in Monaco. People poured into the principality as never before, and it enjoyed its most prosperous season for years. "It is almost impossible to describe the flow of visitors," said one newspaper report. "The Rock of Monaco resembles the Tower of Babel. Pilgrims come from many lands to see the cathedral where Grace was wed and the palace where she gave her wedding breakfast. They cluster round the harbour where Grace started on her honeymoon to see the yacht which carried her off. . ."

Not everyone was pleased by this terrific influx. Monaco's amenities — not least its bars — were swamped by newcomers, and the townspeople became irritable. Nor were their tempers improved by the fact that for the first few weeks the Princess made herself very scarce, hardly appearing in public, and thus disappointing the thousands who came hoping to catch a glimpse of her. Little allowance was made for the fact that Grace was struggling to come to terms with the heat of the Mediterranean summer and the strangeness of her surroundings.

Still more disappointing was the lack of any news about a baby: the people wanted their Princess to become pregnant instantly, so urgent was the principality's need for an heir. Normally, they agreed, it would have been indelicate to show such keen interest in an essentially private matter; but in this case they felt it was excusable, since so many fortunes and businesses were at stake. In the City of London, brokers began working out premiums for customers who wanted to insure against the possibility of no heir being born, and in Monaco itself speculation revived about the so-called Curse of the Grimaldis, which was supposed to have blighted the Royal family's marriages in past generations. Would Princess Grace be strong enough and wise enough to ward off the ghosts which had plagued her husband's ancestors?

Not until August were the spectres laid. Then, over the radio on August 2nd, Rainier broadcast news of "a great and joyous event." The Princess was expecting a child next February. "It is a great joy for me to associate you all in our new happiness," said the Prince. "This must reinforce our hope in the future."

His optimism proved justified. Everyone relaxed: instead of demanding public appearances, people became protective and wished the Princess success in this, the most important of her tasks.

In September 1956 the Royal couple crossed the Atlantic to visit Grace's family, and in October they were received at the White House in Washington by President Eisenhower. In her absence the Princess was elected President of the Monaco Red Cross — an office which she filled with exceptional energy, imagination and distinction for the rest of her life.

Immediate attention, however, was focussed on the all-important baby, rather than on charitable works. Gamblers in the casino punted heavily on the sex of the unborn baby: for every five who put their money on it being a girl, seven bet on a boy. On

The Princess with green fingers: Grace in the 16th Century splendour of the Grimaldi Royal Palace.

Another US President: Princess Grace and her husband pay a social call on "Ike" at the White House.

On May 24th, 1961, President John F. Kennedy entertained Prince Rainier and Princess Grace to a small lunch at the White House in Washington.

The climax of the State visit to Eire in June 1961. Grace arrives at Dublin Castle for a reception with Sean Lemass, President of Eire, and Mrs de Valera, wife of the Irish Prime Minister.

A warm embrace from Lord Mountbatten as he and Princess Grace meet aboard the liner CUNARD PRINCESS on a cruise from New York to Bermuda in 1977.

Rome, 1957: the Royal couple are received by the Pope, who granted them a private audience in the Vatican.

89

*"When she came into the room, you looked at no-one else,"
said a man who saw her often in Monaco. "Her beauty was
breathtaking." Grace dressed for a fancy dress ball.*

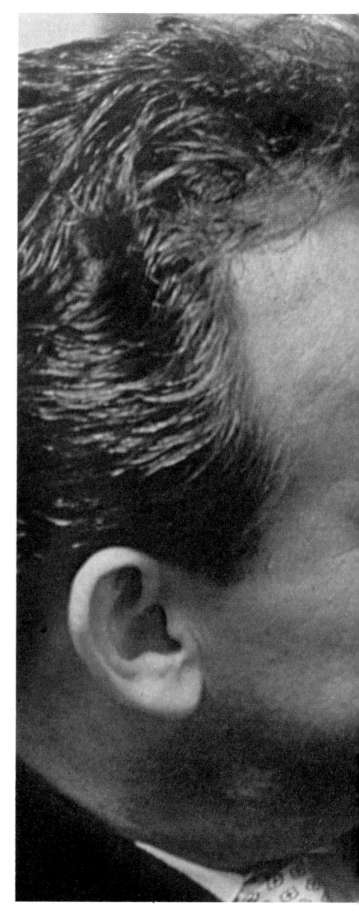

*The looks that capitvated Hollywood and film fans
innumerable made a stunning impact in real life: Grace with
Rainier early in their marriage.*

January 20th, 1957 there was a false alarm and a flurry of excitement when the harbour guns began a twenty-one gun salute, but it was soon established that the firing was in honour of the Sultan of Morocco, who had come on a State visit.

At last the great day came: at 9.27 on the morning of Wednesday, January 23rd 1957, in a converted library overlooking the Palace gardens, the Princess was safely delivered of an 8lb 3oz girl, "in the natural manner and without anaesthetics."

The baby was named Caroline Louise Marguerite. Her father, on the radio, gave thanks to God that "all passed off well," and the town went wild with excitement. A twenty-one gun salute was begun, but in true comic opera fashion the elderly guns functioned erratically, and stuttered to a halt after only seventeen (or, some said, nineteen) rounds had been fired. Church bells rang. Sirens and whistles sounded. Red and white bunting sprouted, red and white carnations were rushed out on to window sills and balconies. In bars and restaurants free champagne was served. The succession was ensured.

In no other European state are the personal affairs of the ruler so closely connected with politics. Just as the announcement of Rainier's engagement had vaporised a swelling wave of opposition the year before, so now the birth of the baby put the whole

Both before and after her marriage, Grace was tireless in her fund-raising. She took particular trouble to help children and old people. Here (in 1955) she joined the "March of Dimes" fashion show at the Waldorf Astoria Hotel in New York to raise funds for polio research.

country in a sunny mood.

With the later birth of Prince Albert, on March 14th 1958, the future was made doubly secure. Although Princess Caroline had been declared the heiress-presumptive, it had always been known that she would yield precedence if her mother bore a son. So now Albert became the heir, and the birth of a boy touched off a fresh bout of celebration: a salute of 101 guns (all fired, apparently!) and festivities throughout the principality.

Albert's christening led to another unseemly outburst from Sir Bernard and Lady Docker, who, when invited to the ceremony, asked if they might bring along their son Lance, whose nineteenth birthday fell on the same day. Reasonably enough, the Palace answered that everything had been carefully worked out, and there were no spare places. At this Lady Docker, a relentless exhibitionist, first refused

She still wore long white gloves — as here, at an official reception — but the image of the demure Miss Kelly had been replaced by one far grander.

On the tennis court she cut a trim, athletic figure, and played with a natural flair inherited in her Kelly genes.

to go to the christening at all, and then aired her views at a Press conference in the Hotel Majestic at Cannes.

Next day, back in Monte Carlo, she became involved in an unsavoury incident, whose exact nature varied when different people described it. According to Sir Bernard, all that happened was that as they got up to leave their table after a meal in the restaurant of the Hotel de Paris, she knocked a small Monegasque flag out of the bowl of flowers in which it had been standing, and threw it on the floor in an outburst of irritation over the way she had been insulted by Rainier. According to the waiters, by contrast, she picked the flag out of the bowl and deliberately tore it in two before hurling it on the

Even when wearing a towel turban and a swimsuit, and snapped doing her make-up, she retained an unmistakable elegance and poise.

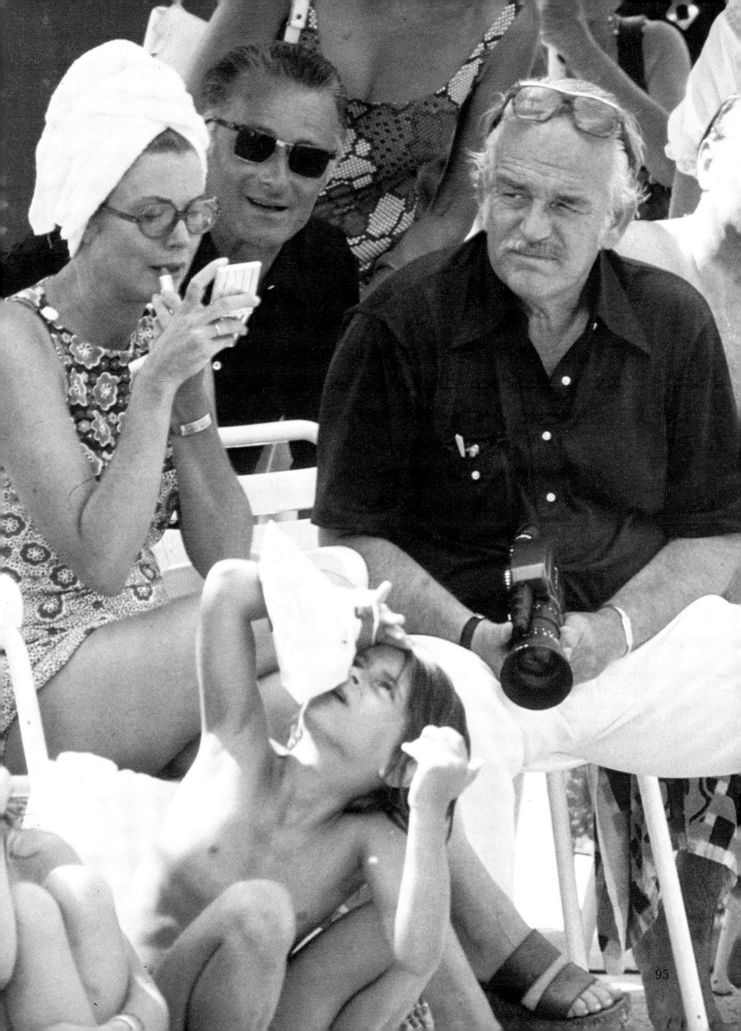

*In Nice with her old friend the actor David Niven and a
Russian ballet dancer then relatively new to the west, Rudolf
Nureyev: August 1963.*

floor, crying out that she would not be needing it.
All she achieved (apart from a vast amount of
publicity) was to bring ridicule on herself, and sever
her connection with the Palace, although for years
she tried to reopen relations, the Prince would never
accept her overtures.

Now that they had two children, Grace and
Rainier felt still more strongly the need for a home
less formal than the Palace — a smaller house, in
which they could relax, off-duty, and be themselves.
They therefore found a site at Roc Agel, in the
mountains above Monte Carlo, and built themselves
a villa on a rocky spur, where a farmhouse had once
stood, commanding tremendous views of the sea.
French newspapers often referred to the house as
their ''ranch'' or new ''mountain palace'', but in
fact it was quite modest: often, when visitors called,
Rainier himself would answer the door. There
Grace kept animals and grew vegetables — an echo
of her childhood labours in Philadelphia. Indoors,
the family had room to spread itself — the children
with their toys and later with their stereo systems,

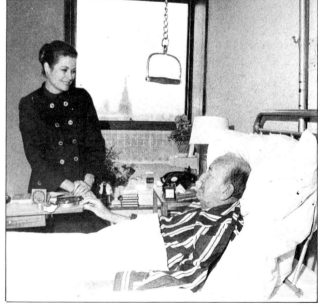

*On November 17th, 1970, Princess Grace visited Noel
Coward in St. Thomas's Hospital, London, where he was
recovering from pleurisy. The night before, she had deputised
for him at a charity show in the Royal Festival Hall. The
master was delighted: never, he said, had he had a more
beautiful understudy.*

Two-year-old Princess Stephanie seems unimpressed by Fred Astaire on the set of Finian's Rainbow *in Hollywood to which Princess Grace paid a nostalgic visit in 1967.*

Echoes of show-business: the Princess with Sharee and Henry Fonda at a ceremonial drink.

she with her dried-flower pressing, he with his metal work. She was never happier than when wandering on the mountains in search of unusual flowers, either for preservation or for planting in the garden.

Gardening, for which she had a lifelong passion, was one of the activities that kept her in the public eye on an easy, practical level. Having founded the Monaco Garden Club in 1968, she was often organising flower shows and competitions, many of them designed to raise money for charity.

The amount of fund-raising which she did for charities was enormous, and widely appreciated; so was the energy which she put into various community projects. Whether she was galvanising the Red Cross, reorganising an old people's home, promoting local arts and crafts through her own Princess Grace Foundation, or cherishing the Monaco ballet school, she continuously endeared herself to her subjects by her genuine concern about their welfare.

Gradually, with the sure touch which had characterised her whole career, Grace began to establish herself in her role as Princess. She met minor antagonism from some of the principality's most deeply entrenched aristocrats, who thought that no American woman, however special, was good enough for them. But soon all reasonable people saw that she exercised a profoundly beneficial influence on Rainier. They saw, to their fascination, that on social occasions she was the dominant partner, the stronger character. He, adoring her, and being essentially gentle, was content to stand back

Off-duty at Roc Agel, their mountain farm, Grace and Rainier could escape from the pressures of formal life. She was never happier than when walking on the hill-side in search of wild flowers.

99

and let her lead.

Whether or not her domination and influence extended to political matters was a question for lively debate; but many Monegasques believed that she was at least indirectly responsible for some of the most important decisions and reforms.

One *cause célèbre* of the early 1960s was the question of the live pigeon-shooting, a cruel and archaic sport much venerated in Monaco. (The pigeons, with feathers clipped to make them fly erratically, were mown down by the competitors, and many fell wounded into the sea or on to the terrace of the Hotel de Paris). Rainier, it was said, had long wanted to get it stopped, but had not had the nerve to impose a ban, such was the mystique surrounding it: the names of cup-winners were recorded in gold lettering in the club room, and included grandees from many countries. The fact that it did suddenly come to an end was widely attributed to Princess Grace, who could not bear a pastime so callous and artificial to flourish on her territory.

Another success credited to her was the ending of the siege laid on Monaco by General de Gaulle in 1962 and 1963. In an attempt to force French tax laws on the principality, the President had erected makeshift customs barriers on the frontier roads, and had threatened to cut off the electricity supply. After months of acrimony and tension, Rainier and Grace dined with de Gaulle one night in Paris, and the main points of the dispute were quickly settled. Afterwards Rainier confided to a friend that he had found it impossible to get through to the General, who had talked entirely in lofty clichés. The only person who did score a success with him was Grace. Even if she did no more than charm him into a more malleable frame of mind, she gave her husband invaluable support.

Again, when Monaco was still going downhill, and Onassis was proposing to close more and more of its amenities, it was she who stepped in to prevent him disbanding the orchestra. This one intercession was later seen as the turning point in the principality's fortunes: thereafter, it began to regain its *chic*.

The fact is that throughout the twenty-six years of Grace's reign, both the image and the stability of Monaco improved dramatically. From being a seedy gambling resort living on the splendours of the past, half ridiculous and half sinister, the principality transformed itself into a thriving business community, with a formidably efficient police force (in which it took particular pride) and the lowest crime statistics of any town on the Riviera.

What part did Grace play in this transformation? At the least she steadied her husband, whose political reactions had been notoriously volatile, and thus forestalled a number of potentially damaging rows. She became a trusted partner with whom he could discuss problems and try out ideas. Yet there is also evidence that her role was often more positive than this. According to one of her friends, it was she who persuaded Rainier not to let the international financier Adnan Khashoggi set up his European headquarters in Monaco, on the grounds that the presence of an operator with such a record (particularly in the field of arms dealing) would do Monaco's name no good. Nearer home, she would have nothing to do with the Pastor family — one of the richest in the principality — who bought up land on the seafront, built skyscrapers there, and always sought to cultivate Rainier's friendship.

Yet perhaps her greatest contribution to Monaco's stability was the personal example which she herself set. Simply by showing her subjects that she was a warm, practical and patently *good* woman

Old comrades reunite: Princess Grace with Cary Grant in 1980.

— a mother bringing up a family — she somehow humanised the whole place and made it real again. Simply by pressing on with ordinary life in an unassuming way, she pulled Monaco back from the brink of unreality and gave it a sense of purpose. By being herself, she transcended the Ruritanian image.

To outsiders, it seemed that she made the transition from film-star to princess with extraordinary ease. Certainly she gave no hint of over-reaching herself or giving herself artificial airs: her sturdy, thoroughbred character enabled her to absorb the multiple pressures and work away industriously at what she saw as a new job.

Yet she did not find it as simple as she made it appear. In later interviews she admitted that she had been homesick at first, and had found it hard to get used to the rigidities of Monegasque protocol. One deprivation with which she had had to come to terms was the loss of liberty: no longer could she walk along the street or go out shopping unrecognised. Being basically a shy person, she said, she did not like being thrown into contact with strangers, but she simply had to master this aversion.

On formal occasions she was every inch a Princess — stunningly attractive, wonderfully dressed, her looks heightened by marvellous jewellery — and her demeanour was suitably dignified. Yet what really endeared her to the people of Monaco was the way she relaxed when *off* duty, moving among them with a pleasing informality.

Nowhere did she behave more naturally than on the golf course at Mont Agel, a couple of kilometres from Roc Agel. Often she would arrive there unannounced and play with a marvellous inborn athleticism, using a straight, flat, flailing swing as if she were batting at baseball. Sometimes she would play with the Director of the Club, sometimes with her husband, and often with her children. If Rainier was present, the game would be far less amusing, for he was always a stilted player, with none of her natural flair.

So keen was she to take exercise that often she would come up by herself for half an hour on the practice fairway. Inevitably word would go round that someone special had arrived, and the edges of the practice ground would become lined with gawping spectators, many of them American tourists.

A royal but private joke as Rainier whispers into Grace's ear.

When a friend tried to correct her style by saying, ''Ma'am — that's a *baseball* swing,'' she replied with a disarming smile, ''That's too bad. It's the way I *like* to swing!''

Sometimes she caused still greater consternation by actually organising a game of baseball on the golf course. When US Navy ships came into harbour at Nice, some of the crewmen would drive up for a round of golf, only to find themselves being hijacked into a game of baseball by an amazingly attractive blonde in very short shorts. When they realised who it was, they would be temporarily overcome by shock; but so utterly natural was she that they soon recovered and pitched in enthusiastically. ''She was so marvellous with them that in five minutes it was just a case of Miss Kelly playing with her brothers,'' said a friend who often saw her there. ''In her shorts and blue baseball cap, she looked an absolute knockout. On the front of her cap was a big silver M, and once, when I asked her what it meant, she said, 'It stands for Mum!' ''

On many occasions after golf or baseball she would decline offers of a lift home and insist on walking back, in spite of the heat and the ever present possibility of a kidnap attempt. ''No, thanks,'' she would say. ''I'll go on my own. I want to think.'' And off she would stride, across the links and down the winding road.

At the Olympic-size swimming pool which she and Rainier built for the principality on the edge of the harbour, she would plunge into the fray with an equal lack of inhibition. One year at the swimming festival she, Albert and Caroline entered for the family relay race. Albert, on the first leg, more or less held his own; on the second Caroline drew

Official duties: the Royal Family of Monaco lead a procession from the Cathedral during a national fete.

Face in the crowd: a Princess roots for her team.

slightly ahead; and on the third Grace forged away to win by a distance — all with no loss of dignity.

Everyone lucky enough to have been a guest at the Palace confirms that she was a wonderful hostess. "Her beauty was breathtaking," recalls one man who knew the Royal couple well. "This, backed by her dignity, gave her enormously powerful magnetism. When she came into a room, you looked at no one else."

And yet she always retained her own way of doing things. Guests invited to lunch or dinner would find they got nothing to drink until their hostess arrived in the room. Then, when a drink was served, it might be very strange — a pineapple cocktail crusted with powdered nuts, or some other bizarre concoction about which she had read in a magazine. No matter how exotic, the brew was usually delicious, and in abundant supply.

Friends enjoyed most the evenings on which she gave "small" dinner parties. Perhaps twenty people would sit down to a delicious meal, and afterwards they would watch a new film, not yet released. Although some of the guests might be local worthies, invited out of duty, they would be leavened by friends of the highest calibre: the Nivens, the Mountbattens, the Oliviers.

Even for people who knew her well, however, it was not always safe to relax, as she was liable to spring after-dinner surprises. One night, to their consternation, guests found themselves ushered into the Grand Hall of the Castle, which was full from end to end with huge buckets of flowers. Their hostess announced an impromptu flower-arranging competition, in which everybody present was required to compete: each man and woman was given a vase and half an hour. The blow was softened by the fact that Grace herself would be the judge, and by the generosity of the prizes offered; but no excuses were accepted, and no one was allowed to escape.

On her own territory she could be extremely bossy: she knew what she wanted, and got it. But she was always so natural and unaffected that people hardly ever resented it when she told them what to do.

One subject of never-ending speculation was the possibility that she might one day return to film-making. Even with her new career firmly established and her family started, many people still could not accept that she had abandoned professional acting for ever. What they failed to realise was that even at the height of her Hollywood fame and success she had never regarded film-making as the be-all and end-all of her life. As Donald Sinden correctly divined, she had always wanted a family.

"I always knew that one day I would marry," she

Poetry-readings gave Princess Grace a new intellectual outlet as she approached her 50th birthday — a way of returning to the theatre without loss of dignity. "Whenever she came on stage," said her director John Carroll, "a rustle went through the audience."

A growing interest in conservation led Princess Grace to stop wearing wild animal furs, and to support the World Wildlife Fund.

said in a later interview. "I also knew that I would then have to give up acting. No one can have a career and a happy family life at the same time. To have a husband and children has always meant more to me than anything else."

All the same, she was bombarded with offers from film companies, the truth was that an enormous amount of people *wanted* her to act again, most of them so that they could simply have the pleasure of watching her, but a few for more professional reasons. One of the first serious attempts to lure her back was made by the Fench producer Jules Borkon, who in 1958 proposed that she should star in what he described as "a deeply religious film", *The Dialogue of the Carmelites.* Borkon went so far as to fly a religious adviser from Chicago to Monaco, trying to persuade Grace to take part, but his overtures came to nothing.

As the years went by, hopes of her making a comeback gradually receded; but then in 1962 came a concrete proposal from the one man with the power to draw her back onto the screen: Alfred Hitchcock. He proposed — and she agreed — that she should play the lead in *Marnie*, a thriller by the British author Winston Graham. Her part was to be that of the name character, a thief who marries to escape a prison sentence. She was to report for work in Hollywood that summer during the two-month holiday which she and Rainier planned to spend in the States.

From the start there were obvious technical problems. Marnie is English, not American, and morally unattractive: a girl from the slums, much given to foul language, with lice in her hair and sexually frigid. Could Grace play such a character convincingly?

No doubt these difficulties could have been overcome. Hitchcock hired the American writer Evan Hunter to produce a script, and Hunter set about converting Marnie into an American, at the same time transferring the scene from England to the United States. Yet already such political and religious opposition was brewing that the idea of Grace participating was doomed to an early death.

First MGM threatened that they might sue Grace if she took the part. She was, the company claimed, still under contract to them, her agreement having been only suspended in 1956, and never cancelled. Soon rumours began to fly that the only reason she wanted to go back into films was that her marriage

was breaking up. Then it was reported that an envoy from the Vatican had called at the Palace in Monaco and conveyed the Pope's hope that she would not set other Catholic families a bad example by leaving her two young children to return to work. The strongest pressure, however, came from the people of Monaco: even though prince Rainier himself had backed Grace's decision — and had proposed to accompany her when she went filming — his subjects made it clear that they thoroughly disliked the plan.

Faced with so much hostility, she and Hitchcock gradually backed down. To disarm criticism she made it known that her $1,000,000 fee would go to charity. Then, in April, it was announced that the project had been deferred until the following spring. In June Grace revealed that the idea had been abandoned altogether, and she was candid enough to admit that one of the reasons was the "unfavourable reaction" of her 24,000 subjects. The moral of the whole episode was clear: the Monegasques wanted their Princess to stay at home. In 1963 she did star in a film — but this was an entirely different matter: a

documentary about Monaco, in which she was the natural centre of attraction.

As Grace herself remarked, one of the compensations for enduring the formalities of official duty, was the foreign travel which her status brought in train. She and Rainier travelled all over the world calling on other Heads of State — President Kennedy in Washington, Queen Elizabeth in London, as well as on others of lesser note.

One of her most emotional trips was the pilgrimage which she and Rainier made to Westport, Co. Mayo, the home of her Irish ancestors, in the summer of 1961. At the news of her coming the little town between the mountains and the sea went into a frenzy of preparation: trees were felled to give a better view of the church, every weed was grubbed up from the central street, the Mall, and so many local people — Kellys, Quinns and Gills — claimed kinship with the Princess that Lord Killanin, Monaco's honorary Consul-General in Ireland, had to go and sort them out, ruling in the

Baseball on the golf-course at Mont Agel during the Monte Carlo centenary festivities of 1966. On less formal occasions, American sailors were amazed when they realised who it was who had press-ganged them into a game.

end that only the nine families of second cousins would be able to meet her.

She had merely to arrive in Dublin to provoke a riot. The crowd outside the Gresham Hotel was so huge and excited that she and Rainier were trapped in their car for fifteen minutes before they could enter the hotel for a banquet. Afterwards, fifty people needed hospital treatment.

Her welcome in Mayo was not much more controlled, and no less joyous. She was mobbed everywhere she went — outside the church in Westport, at tea with Widow Mulchrone (one of the cousins), at the foot of Croagh Patrick, the holy mountain from which St. Patrick is said, by ringing his bell, to have expelled all the snakes from Ireland. But to her undoubtedly the most touching part of the trip was her visit to the remains of a cottage, since used as a byre for cattle and now half buried in grass and rushes, which was believed to have been her grandfather's home. So taken was she with the site that she later returned to it, and always hoped to build a small house there as a holiday home. In 1962 she again met one of the Irishmen who had accompanied her tour, and confessed that although she had enjoyed the trip enormously, she had really never been able to sort out one claimant-cousin from the next!

A more exotic journey was the one she made in 1971 to Teheran and Persepolis, where she and Rainier joined in Persia's 2,500th anniversary celebrations. At a cost estimated to be between £50 and £100 million, the Shah invited nearly all the world's crowned heads and leading statesmen, and housed them all in a glittering tented city on the plain beneath the floodlit ruins of Cyrus the Great's capital. The festival was an extraordinary mixture of pomp, pageantry and politics, all the statesmen being encouraged to discuss their problems with each other between the banquets and ceremonies; but for Grace, with her strong sense of history, it was thrilling enough to feel the pulse of a site so famous, and she quoted to one of her fellow guests the golden lines from Marlowe's *Tamburlaine*:

Is it not passing brave to be a king
And ride in triumph through Persepolis?

Next year, 1972, she and her husband flew to Budapest for an earthier celebration: Elizabeth Taylor's fortieth birthday party, thrown by her husband of the day, Richard Burton, at which stars of stage and screen congregated from all over the world. Burton's present to his wife as at least as spectacular as any of the gifts which had been bestowed on Grace by her Prince and people: a diamond presented in 1621 by the Moghul emperor Shah Jehan to his wife Mumtaz Mahal, in whose memory he later built the Taj Mahal.

To former colleagues on stage and screen, Grace remained a perennially faithful friend. In 1971, for instance, when Frank Sinatra said farewell to show business, she flew to Los Angeles and went on stage at the Music Center to praise him and Hollywood — "not so much the glamorous Hollywood, but the hard-work Hollywood: the getting-up at five a.m. and worrying about the next job." The show — to which her presence made no small contribution, was a highly-charged occasion and reduced many of Hollywood's most seasoned campaigners to tears. It was also an enormous financial success, raising more than 800,000 dollars for charity.

Afterwards Grace much enjoyed telling a little story about a conversation she had had in the plane on the way to Los Angeles. The man in the seat next to her kept telling her at length about his family and children. She, wanting neither to offend him nor to let on who she was, made polite, non-committal replies. Unabashed, her neighbour brought out photographs of his children and continued to sing their praises. At last, when they landed, he asked what it was that had brought her to Los Angeles. She muttered something about coming to do a benefit show - whereupon he stared at her and said, "Oh — I thought you'd stopped being an actress and become a princess."

Whenever she came to London she would ring Donald Sinden, who played in *Mogambo* with her, and suggest a meal or a drink; and although he could never quite take seriously the way she announced herself on the telephone as "Grace de Monaco", he was always thrilled to see her. To Sinden, in her role as First Lady of Monaco she was still playing a part: "She saw the part of Princess *as* a part, and when she was on duty she played it to perfection. She knew it was the best part she had ever had in her life."

Off duty, she was the same as ever: unassuming, friendly, a splendid mimic, always ready for fun. One night she arrived unannounced to see the play *London Assurance*, in which Sinden had the lead. What she did not know was that she had come on Judi Dench's birthday, and that the cast had clubbed together (as they did for everyone's anniversary) to buy her a present, which was to be given her later that evening.

After the performance, as Grace came through the pass-door to the back of the stage, Sinden met her and in a few moments explained what was happening. Without hesitation she agreed to make the presentation, thereby enabling him to bring off a spectacular entrance to the assembled cast: he was so fed up with making these presentations himself, he said, that at vast expense he had flown in someone special. . .

8

THE FAMILY

Having always loved children, Grace was delighted by the arrivals of Caroline, Albert, and (in February 1965) Stephanie. Soon the family became one of the greatest pleasures she and Rainier shared. It was therefore all the more painful for her when Caroline grew up to be a rebellious teenager and — as if resurrecting the old curse on Grimaldi happiness — made a disastrous marriage.

In her own childhood Grace had sometimes felt deprived of attention, so much time did her mother spend away from home championing the cause of women in medicine. Admirable though Ma Kelly's motives no doubt were, they left a scar on her second daughter, and Grace herself was determined not to make the same mistake with her own family.

The result was that she gave the children an enormous amount of time and care, and perhaps — with the best of intentions — overdid it. Certainly Caroline, looking back, felt she had been over-cossetted. "By the time we reached our teens, we all longed for some kind of action," she wrote in a magazine article. "It was not only boring: we were too protected. At sixteen we felt out of touch with the rest of the world."

Soon after Albert's birth the Princess took on an English nanny, Maureen King, but instead of consigning their infants and minder to the nursery, Grace and Rainier spent every possible moment with them. Though they tried to be strict, they were

Royal family, royal home: Princess Grace and Prince Rainier with Stephanie, Albert and Caroline on the grand staircase in the courtyard of the Grimaldi Palace.

in fact fairly indulgent parents, and in material things at least the children became spoiled. "She had everything," recalled Caroline's closest childhood friend Helen Faggionato. "Play kitchens that cooked, play cars that drove, live animals and stuffed animals and everything."

Caroline grew up lively and bright, bilingual in English and French. At fourteen she left her private convent school in Monaco and went to board for two years at St. Mary's, Ascot, the exclusive girls' school in England where instruction in social etiquette formed an important part of the curriculum. But she did not waste time learning to curtsey: after only two years at St. Mary's she passed three A-levels, in French, English, and Spanish — no mean achievement for somebody landed in a foreign environment. After that she returned to Paris, where she went to Les Dames de St. Maur, a private school, to study for her *baccalauréat*.

Already, aged seventeen, she was exceptionally attractive, with her mother's blue eyes and clearcut features and her father's olive complexion. But she wielded a far more overt sexuality than her mother: no snow-maiden, she had become precocious, outspoken, and wayward.

Once the Press decided she was newsworthy and latched on to her, she got no respite: wherever she stayed or was expected, cameramen were lurking. Unlike her mother, who had learned to deal with this kind of thing during her years in Hollywood, she allowed herself to be snapped in compromising situations, wearing provocative clothes — exactly the sort of traps which Grace had assiduously avoided.

Columns of gossip were published about her boyfriends. For years papers kept up the suggestion that she would make a good wife for Prince Charles. There was even a brief attempt to link her name with that of Ahmed Fuad, son of the late ex-King Farouk of Egypt: but he, unlike his flamboyant father, had early learnt the value of discretion. One look at his Albanian bodyguard was enough to send the Press slinking home.

Worse still, newsmen got wind of the fact that Caroline was at odds with her mother, who still wanted to keep her on a short rein. Grace often proclaimed her belief that the home should be ''an oasis for the family'', a place in which they could all find ''a sense of well-being and strength, replenishment and renewal.'' It hurt her deeply when Caroline began to say that she could not stand the suffocating cocoon of Monaco any longer.

A serious rift opened up in 1975 when Caroline, then eighteen, began going around with Philippe Laville, a pop singer ten years older. For him, all news was good news: publicity — whether pro or anti — helped promote his music, and when he was invited to join Monaco's ruling family in a summer cruise round the Greek islands, he seemed to be riding high. But at the last minute, when the disappointing results of Caroline's first year's exams at the Paris Institute of Political Sciences became known, the invitation was withdrawn and Laville was left onshore.

For a few weeks attention shifted to the Swedish tennis champion, Bjorn Borg, who became front-runner in the stakes organised by the Press for Caroline's suitors. But soon after the cruise on the family yacht she began to be seen around Paris nightspots with a second Philippe — Philippe Junot, son of the president in France of the American Westinghouse Corporation. Junot was not ten but seventeen years her senior. He was small, dapper; a man-about-town who claimed descent from Napoleon's secretary, an unabashed *boulevardier* and playboy.

Grace could not approve of such an entanglement. When advice failed to wean her daughter from this utterly unsuitable attachment, she tried tough tactics and even packed her off to America — but Junot followed. Her efforts, and those of Prince Rainier, were unavailing: Caroline was in love. As a minor she could not marry without her parents' consent; but by then she was nearly twenty-one and, with Kelly blood flowing in her veins, she was prepared to wait.

When, after a year, her resolve remained unchanged, Grace and Rainier had no option but to put the best face they could on it and give their blessing to the marriage. Grace made it clear both to her daughter and to outsiders that she would rather have

The birth of Princess Caroline on January 23rd, 1957, was hailed in Monaco with great rejoicing — and a 21-gun salute — since it safeguarded the Principality from annexation by France.

seen Caroline wait a bit longer before taking such an important choice in her life. Being Catholics, the family considered marriage a very serious commitment. Undeterred by these doubts, Caroline still insisted on marrying Junot.

The wedding, held in Monaco in the summer of 1978, was a relatively low-key affair, ostensibly because Rainier and Grace did not want a repeat of the bally-hoo that had accompanied their own star-studded marriage. Once again there were two services on consecutive days. The civil ceremony took place in the Palace throne room where, wearing an ice-blue dress by Dior, the bride made her responses to the formal, black-suited figure of M. Louis Roman, Registrar to the Ruling Family. Her witnesses were her brother, Prince Albert, then twenty, and Grace Levine, an American first cousin.

After the ceremony M. Roman said: ''It was all

very moving. The bride's mother cried and even the bridegroom had tears glistening on his cheeks. Princess Caroline was very nervous.''

The religious wedding the following day also took place in the privacy of the Palace, and although the bride and bridegroom then walked through the narrow streets to give Monegasques a look at her white organdie dress and veil by Dior, and to receive their present of a chest of silver cutlery, Prince Rainier's ban on photographers using helicopters to take pictures of either ceremony was ninety-nine per cent effective. The only breach of the defences was made by a red hang-glider which swooped briefly over the Palace to the accompaniment of cheers from the crowd.

The yacht with which the bride's parents had presented their daughter and new son-in-law — a forty-two foot catamaran — had been delayed in its journey through the Canal du Midi because a twenty-mile stretch was closed for repairs. But it had been rescued by a crane in time to take the couple on their honeymoon cruise.

Grace put a brave face on the wedding but, as she

Prince Albert made his first camera appearance at the age of four days. Born on March 14th, 1958, he had his mother's blue eyes, but chestnut hair.

must have feared all along, it did not last. Only two years later the couple separated, and the snide newspaper comments were as hard to bear as the knowledge that her daughter had failed to measure up to her own high standards. Nevertheless, she welcomed Caroline home with open arms and defended her whenever she saw an opportunity. She said on Mike Douglas' American TV show, ''It's been tough on my children having to live their lives in the constant glare of world publicity. But it's been toughest of all on Caroline, particularly just before and just after her wedding. She's been really victimised by it all. She's overcome it all, though, and she faces everything admirably.''

Caroline had grown up a forceful, independent character: in the classic response of a child whose parent is a super-achiever, she made herself as different from her mother as she possibly could. Her brushes with the Press seemed an outcome of her

By the time Princess Stephanie was christened in 1965, Caroline was already eight and Albert six.

attitude towards publicity. She did not court it, but at the same time she scorned to avoid it. This provoked newsmen to greater efforts, and a love-hate relationship developed in which no holds were barred. Yet the very fact that she constantly attracted attention showed just how much she possessed of that elusive, not always comfortable attribute, Star Quality.

Gradually it became apparent that this could serve her well, if only she learnt to use it as a servant rather than a master. It also seemed possible that the restless playgirl image with which she had been saddled was the result of not having any sufficiently demanding occupation. Coming from two families renowned for energy and hard work, she needed hard work to do. Her family was delighted — but not surprised — when she made a notable success of the job of heading Monaco's UNICEF Year of the Child charity campaign in 1979: for some time they

Princess Grace read aloud to the children from an early age.

had believed that if she were assigned a difficult and demanding job with which she could really identify, her image might change dramatically.

Her brother Albert, heir to the Grimaldi dynasty, though little more than a year younger, came through his childhood in the same glare of world publicity but with very different results.

He seemed to have inherited his mother's invaluable talent for avoiding adverse comment — or indeed much comment at all. Physically, he took after her family, being tall, fair, of athletic build, with the square Kelly jaw and a tendency to short sight. He was a particularly amiable and co-operative child: once, to illustrate the differences in character of her children, Grace told a friend that she seemed to be forever spanking Caroline but scarcely ever punished Albert. She only had to raise her voice slightly and he would obey. As for her younger daughter, Princess Stephanie, she added, she gave up spanking altogether: she could have ''beaten her like a gong'', and it would have made no difference. But this tough talk should surely be taken with a pinch of salt. Grace was an exceptionally patient mother, more inclined to reason with naughty children than to spank them.

Prince Rainier did not wish his son to suffer the difficulties he himself had experienced from being taught in a foreign language, with a foreign system of measures, before learning them in his mother tongue. So Albert was spared exile in English prep and public schools, and instead went to French lycées until he was old enough to move on to Amherst College in America (he had earlier spent a few months in the United States, teaching swimming at summer camp). His father chose a period of training in the French navy as the final stage in his preparation for the task of succeeding to the throne of Monaco.

In public, as in private, Albert always showed an in-built courtesy and gentleness which protected him from sniping even by the Continental Press and made his younger sister Stephanie call him unequivocally, ''the nicest boy in the world.''

As if to prove herself different in every way from her sister, Stephanie made her own public image that of a complete tomboy. Her lively, chubby face was frequently seen making grimaces at Press cameras, and she gave little sign of interest in the usual teenage preoccupations of complexion, figure, clothes and the opposite sex. Wearing jeans and a T-shirt and scorning make-up, she nevertheless, at seventeen, promised to become every bit as attractive as Caroline.

Her education was not without its moments of drama. At the age of sixteen she was asked to leave the Catholic school of St. Dominique de Neuilly for breaking too many of its rules against smoking, rock music and lights after midnight, but when she was transferred to a more liberal establishment where such things were permitted, she showed her appreciation by working hard enough to pass her *baccalauréat* on schedule.

Both Rainier and Grace would have loved to have another child, and in the summer of 1967 they happily announced that she was expecting a fourth baby early in the New Year. Soon after that they travelled to Canada to visit the Montreal Expo '67, taking the whole family and stopping in London (to interview nannies) and Liverpool on the way. In Canada, however, Grace began to feel ill, and she had to cancel a proposed visit to Quebec City. She went into the Royal Victoria Hospital in Montreal, and miscarried the baby. Although she recovered her health quickly, there was never another announcement about further increases in the Monaco ruling family.

She grew older gracefully — there is no other word for it — and in her forties she was still memorably beautiful. One writer who first met her in 1972, when Grace was forty-three, analysed the fascination of her face as lying in ''the juxtaposition of nose and upper lip: she has a little muzzle like some delicate rare creature.''

Not everyone fell victim to her spell. Some men, though admiring her looks, felt that she really *was* no more than a dumb blonde, with very little presence. What they failed to realise was that behind the cool façade an active mind was working.

Some glimpses of her intellectual calibre were given in *My Book of Flowers*, a handsomely illustrated volume which she published with the help of Gwen Robyns in 1980. Not only did the book celebrate her lifelong infatuation with flowers: it also showed how widely she had read in search of literary and historical references. From Shakespeare to Masefield, from Robert Burns to Robert Frost, she made use of many telling quotations. Other passages showed how she had drawn inspiration from John Clare, Jane Austen, Henry Thoreau and others. In her historical survey of the use of herbs for culinary and medicinal purposes she displayed no mean erudition.

The book also gave a striking insight into the importance that flower arranging held for her. At first, she wrote, she and her friends all felt ''nervous and incompetent — which of course we were. But this was only in the beginning, for it became the first step towards the awakening of many hidden talents.

Light dresses for the ladies, dark suits for the gentlemen, as the Royal Family goes walkabout in Monaco.

Tension in the family ranks as Princess Grace waits during a swimming gala with the tomboyish Stephanie and the more sophisticated Caroline.

Prince Albert, here greeting his mother, grew up taller than either of his parents, but his hair started receding when he was in his early twenties.

Princess Caroline's sexuality was far more overt than her mother's had ever been. But was it her strict upbringing that made her rebel later on?

By the age of sixteen, Princess Caroline was already a sophisticated, attractive and highly intelligent young woman, bi-lingual in French and English, and with an excellent academic record.

"Through working with flowers we began to discover things about ourselves that had been dormant. We found agility not only with our fingers but with our inner eyes in searching for line, scale and harmony. In bringing out these talents within ourselves we gained a dimension that enabled us not only to search for harmony in an arrangement, but also to discover the importance of carrying it into our lives and homes."

Equally therapeutic, Grace found, was her hobby of making pressed-flower pictures, and the book described in loving detail how she went about it. The garden room at Roc Agel would always be full of flowers drying in various kinds of improvised presses — usually old telephone books or wads of blotting paper held down by antique flat-irons. In spite of the clutter, she had a kind of "radar instinct" which told her what kinds of flower were where. Seldom, she wrote, did she begin a picture with a preconceived idea; rather, it was like doing a jigsaw (a favourite pastime during her childhood.) As she moved the flowers around, the central image gradually fell into place: "As the design begins to take shape, you get the same feeling of tranquillity as doing needlework. No wonder the Victorian ladies became so skilled in this art."

Wherever she was, she was busy. She complained about her days being too full for her to accomplish everything she wanted. The problem, she would say, was that she was the sort of person who liked to do one thing at a time, properly, "and usually I find I have to do six as best I can."

More and more of her energy was devoted to fund-raising for charity, not merely at home in Monaco, but in England and the United States as well. Just as Ma Kelly had agreed to write a series of gossipy articles about her daughter (which annoyed Grace at the time) provided the fee for them was paid to her favourite charity, the Women's Hospital and Medical College in Philadelphia, so Grace was prepared to write a piece for *Playboy*, as long as the money for it went to a worthwhile cause.

In her advocacy of breast-feeding, in her campaign against pornography, in the strict upbringing of her children, in her decision to give up wearing animal furs, she showed a didactic streak — and indeed Rainier once said that if she could have lived her life over again, she would have liked to be a teacher.

To the very end of her life French and Italian newspapers continued to float scandalous stories that the marriage was on the point of break-up. Like the reports that she was being treated for cancer, these were without foundation, fantasies erected on the fact that she spent a good deal of time at the family apartment in Paris, especially when the girls were at school in the French capital. Nobody blamed her for wanting to escape from Monaco now and then: as she herself said, the place was like a goldfish bowl, in which every movement of every fish was closely observed, and although she got used to the continual scrutiny, to leave it behind for a while was always a relief.

If she and Rainier had one big fear, it was not that they would be separated, but that their fat little capitalist principality would fall victim to some socialist takeover. Only with their closest friends would they discuss these anxieties, but when France turned sharply to the left with the election of François Mitterand as President in 1981, their dread of Communism became painfully apparent.

In his attempts to preserve the family's privacy and dignity, Rainier fought many bitter legal battles with the Press, sometimes winning damages but often not achieving much satisfaction. In a way Grace had become public property.

In 1977 Twentieth-Century Fox TV made a 75-minute documentary about her, *Once Upon a Time. . . Is Now The Story of Princess Grace.* The title alone suggested that the film would contain a high proportion of sugar, and even before it was shown the team that made it was scattered in disarray. Budd Schulberg, who wrote the script, insisted that his name be removed from the credits, and Alec Guinness was excluded. The programme contained no comment from Grace's former boyfriends — Ray Milland, Oleg Cassini, Jean-Pierre Aumont — and even Bing Crosby was not consulted. Not surprisingly, the film was dismissed as a fairy-tale, not to be taken seriously.

In 1981 the American company ABC Television announced to her dismay that it was going to make a film of her life, with Cheryl Ladd playing the central part. She made an official complaint to the company, claiming that the film would constitute an invasion of her privacy, and she enlisted the help of her old friend and colleague Frank Sinatra to see if he could get the project suppressed. Nevertheless, the film went ahead.

The popular idea that she herself might still return to film-making was never abandoned. In 1976 she did make a kind of return when she joined the board of Twentieth-Century Fox (characteristically announcing that she would use her influence to raise the moral tone of the company's productions: ''I want to bring love and peace back to the screen.'') But as a performer she went no further than to appear as the narrator in *The Children of Theatre Street*, a ninety-minute documentary about the Kirov Ballet School, which was released in 1977.

It was a great joy to her that as she approached her fiftieth birthday she hit on an entirely new form of intellectual outlet: the series of poetry readings

After their religious wedding ceremony, Caroline and her husband showed themselves to the public by walking to the Chapelle de la Misericorde, where she left her wedding bouquet on the altar.

which she began in 1976. Though no bookworm, she had always read widely for pleasure, and now she found a real use for her lifelong love of poetry and prose.

Her involvement started when the British author and director John Carroll was devising a programme for the Edinburgh Festival of 1976 to celebrate the bicentenary of American Independence. Needing a star American name, he approached Princess Grace and was as amazed as he was delighted when she accepted.

Nor was he disappointed by her performance: he found she had an excellent voice, perfect timing, and a ready sense of humour. Such was her success at Edinburgh that he worked out another special programme, in which she appeared at Stratford-upon-Avon in 1977. *A Remembrance for Shakespeare* was given in the Holy Trinity Church at Stratford, and when she arrived she brought with her a rose to lay on the Bard's tomb.

Again she made a great impression, and during the festival the distinguished tenor Peter Pears invited her to take part in the Aldeburgh Festival the following year. Thus she appeared at Aldeburgh as well, along with Pears, the Russian 'cellist Rostropovitch, the harpist Ossian Ellis, and the actors Richard Pasco and John Westbrook. This

Princess Grace with Caroline

In her middle-teens, Princess Stephanie deliberately cultivated a tomboy image, and she was expelled from one school for deliberately flouting its rules.

By the time she was seventeen, Princess Stephanie had emerged from her tomboy phase and was on her way to becoming no less attractive than her elder sister.

time, with Pasco, she played the scene between Jessica and Lorenzo from *The Merchant of Venice*, and also read a letter written by Mozart at the age of thirteen.

Meanwhile, news of her impact at Edinburgh had reached America. In response to invitations from there — and in consultation with her — Carroll devised yet another new entertainment in poetry and prose, *Birds, Beasts and Flowers*, which they took on a tour of Pittsburgh, Minneapolis, Philadelphia (her home territory), Washington, Princeton and Harvard early in 1978. Profits from the readings went to the World Wildlife Fund.

Carroll was overjoyed at capturing so beautiful and intelligent a collaborator. "The good gods endowed her with all the most wonderful gifts," he

said when she went to Aldeburgh. "She has beauty, intelligence and charm. But she is also a very kind and nice person: thoughtful and meticulous." He was most impressed by the way she kept to the schedule she had agreed months before, even though (as it then turned out) Caroline's marriage was only a fortnight away. As for Grace herself, she seemed delighted by the opportunities, however modest, of returning to the stage and using some of the skills which she had laid aside so many years before.

Her final stage performance in England took place on March 16th, 1981 when she gave a reading at Chichester, in Sussex, to launch the Festival Theatre's twenty-first birthday celebrations. Her presence filled every one of the 1,374 seats, and although Chichester's open thrust-stage and large auditorium are not easy for a single performer, she carried off her parts of the programme magnificently. The staff found her a delight to deal with: warm, serene and almost shy about her performance, but at the same time distinguished by an unmistakable aura of royalty. "You felt you would never get very close to her," said one of them. "In spite of being so pleasant, she was definitely a princess."

She and Carroll were full of plans for further readings, the first in the Chapel Royal at Windsor towards the end of September 1982.

She was due back in England on September 27th 1982 to take part in *For this House*, a "mosaic in words and music" to be given in St. George's Chapel, Windsor. As usual, Carroll put the script together and sent it for her comments. In a letter written five days before she died she wrote that she loved the programme: it was the best he had ever done for her.

Carroll decided that, being a thorough professional, she would have wanted the show to go ahead without her, so he brought in the actress Barbara Jefferies to take her place. All the same, her death severed a unique association. Carroll had already planned two more tours for her — one in Salzburg and Munich, the other in America — and she was looking forward to them keenly.

Yet it was the magnetism and warmth of her personality, rather than her skill as an actress, that Carroll will miss most. "Whenever she came on stage, a rustle went through the audience, because she had such radiant beauty and dignity: she really did look like a million dollars. And although she was candid in her criticism, she was the kindest person in the world: I never heard her say a bitchy word about anyone."

The last photograph taken of the united Grimaldi family, shopping in San Remo on September 10th, 1982, only four days before Grace's death.

9

A TRAGIC END

Just before ten o'clock on the morning of Monday, September 13th 1982, Princess Grace left her mountain home, Roc Agel, in her Rover 3500 to drive herself and Stephanie down to the Palace, a journey of about five miles. The road down the face of the mountain — a series of straight stretches ending in hairpin bends — was steep and awkward, but she had driven it hundreds of times before and knew every twist.

At about 10 am the gendarme on duty in the village of La Turbie noticed the car go through normally. But a minute or two later a lorry driver, following it down the hill, saw it start to weave from one side of the tarmac to the other as it approached the last bend before the mountain road joined the main corniche below. Instead of slowing for the corner, the Rover shot out over the hairpin like a missile, plummeted 120 feet down a precipice, turning over and over as it went, smashed through some bushes, and landed in a market garden with such an impact that the owner, Sesto Lequio, thought a

The car finished up on its side, badly crushed. Flames burst out of its engine, but Lequio snatched a fire-extinguisher from his truck and put them out.

Deep in shock, Prince Rainier leads his depleted family party at Princess Grace's funeral on September 18th, 1982. Princess Stephanie, her neck injured in the car crash, was too ill to leave hospital.

The wreck of Princess Grace's Rover 3,500, crushed by its 120-foot fall over a precipice, is recovered by the Monaco police.

Poignantly elegant in black, the Princess of Wales represented Queen Elizabeth at Princess Grace's funeral.

The final hairpin of the Moyenne Corniche, which Princess Grace's car failed to negotiate. The Rover shot out over the edge of the bend where the two women are standing, and plunged into a market garden below.

Then he opened a front door and pulled out Stephanie, who was conscious and lying in the driver's seat. Grace was trapped in the back, hair covering her face. Another man who ran to help shouted "Can you hear me? Can you hear me?" but she did not answer.

Although the crash had happened on French soil Lequio, knowing who the victims were, got his wife to telephone the Royal Palace. In eight minutes the Monaco fire brigade had arrived to cut Grace free. She was rushed to The Princess Grace Hospital, but when she arrived there she was already in what Dr. Jean Chatelin, the chief surgeon, called a "deep coma." In spite of it, he started to work on her at once, setting fractures in collar-bone and right thigh and restoring vital functions. He also telephoned Dr. Jean Duplay, the leading neurologist in Nice, for advice. What he could not do, because the 24-year-old hospital lacked the equipment, was to carry out a brain scan — a procedure which would have been adopted as standard in any modern casualty department with an accident victim of this kind. The only suitable scanner was in a private clinic belonging to

Dr. Michel Mourou, and it was not until the evening, eight hours after the crash, that Grace could be moved there.

Meanwhile the Monaco police had hurried out and recovered the wreck with a breakdown truck, driving it straight back to the Palace. Thus, by the time the French police arrived at the scene of the accident, the evidence had gone.

It happened that the Palace's experienced Press Officer, Nadia Lacoste, was out of the country on holiday. In her absence the Palace issued a highly-misleading statement, which said that the Princess had had an accident and had broken her thigh, that her condition was "stationary", and that the crash appeared to have been caused by mechanical failure.

How this statement was concocted, and why it was put out, never became clear. But it seems that the Press Office, conditioned by years of denying information to importunate inquirers, decided in a panic to put up a smokescreen which would keep newsmen at bay. Yet there was also a strong element of deception in the optimistic bulletin: when Nadia Lacoste rang to ask if she had better come back, she was told that her presence was not needed. All the same, she did return.

British Leyland, the firm which had made the car, at once despatched two engineers to inspect the wreck, but they were refused access to it. Although

The trajectory of the Rover after it had left the road. It smashed down into the vegetable patch with an impact like an aeroplane crashing.

the vehicle was eleven years old, it had done only a low mileage, and the company pointed out that as the car had been equipped with a dual braking-system, it was extremely improbable that both circuits could have failed simultaneously.

The brain scan, performed that evening, confirmed that Grace had suffered a massive haemorrhage from brain injuries. But according to Dr. Duplay it also showed that there had been a separate haemorrhage of a cerebral artery. In other words, she had suffered a stroke, which would have caused giddiness or loss of consciousness. From the medical evidence, and from Stephanie's description of what happened in the car, he deduced that she had had a sudden black-out, which made her lose control of the vehicle, but that this minor stroke would not necessarily have been fatal if she had not been driving at the time. The main brain damage had been inflicted by blows sustained during the crash. Stephanie — said by the Palace bulletin to be only bruised — had in fact sustained concussion and a serious fracture of the backbone.

During Monday night Grace's condition deteriorated. By Tuesday morning she was being kept alive only by heart and lung machines. Chatelin and Duplay agreed that nothing could be done to save her: even a trepanning operation would have been ineffective, for her brain was already dead. In the evening Chatelin contacted Rainier, Albert and Caroline, and told them there was no hope. At 9.30 pm they took the terrible decision that the doctors should disconnect the life-support systems. And so Princess Grace died.

When the news went out on Monaco radio, stunned paralysis gripped the Principality. The roulette wheels slowed and stopped; the casinos closed. People came out and stood in the streets dumbfounded. All round the world television and radio stations interrupted their programmes to announce that Princess Grace was dead, many of them with a note of incredulity. Next morning, front-page headlines blazed the news across every country. For many people memories swirled back, in nightmare form now, of the desperate car-chase which she had filmed with Hitchcock for *To Catch a Thief*, there on the Riviera, on a serpentine mountain road exactly like the one that had killed her.

The shock was compounded by two factors: one, that a beautiful woman's life had ended prematurely in violence; and two, that the grotesque medical bulletin put out on Monday strongly suggested some form of cover-up on the Palace's part.

Speculation began to seethe. Had the Monaco doctors failed to handle the casualty properly? Why, if the car's brakes were supposed to have failed, had the British Leyland representatives not been allowed to inspect it? Why had the extent of Grace's injuries been concealed? Above all, had Stephanie, who was rescued from the driver's side of the car, been at the wheel when the accident occurred?

At seventeen she was a year too young to hold a French driving licence. But her mother, who was short-sighted and wore contact lenses, had never liked driving, and might have been letting her practise. . . On the contrary, others said: Grace was a highly responsible and law-abiding mother, she would never have let Stephanie drive illegally on that journey, which would have ended in the busy streets of the town, where any number of passers-by might see her.

The uncertainties made local people angry. They felt they had been deceived by the Palace, and they could not see why. They did not realise what a phobia Rainier and his officials had developed about the Press, and so could not imagine that the bulletin had been a misguided attempt to defuse alarm rather than increase it.

Years before, Rainier, fulminating against the menace of Monte Carlo gossip and rumour, had given a strangely prophetic illustration of how news could get out of hand: ''You have a bump with your car. Five minutes later it has become a bad accident. Next it is really dramatic: the car is wrecked and you are injured. It ends with you being thrown out into the road and killed.'' Then, when it actually happened, he had tried at all costs to forestall that kind of progression.

The Principality went into deep mourning. Black ribbons hung everywhere in the Old Town and in Monte Carlo. Above the pink-and-grey Palace the Royal standard drooped at half mast, and bells tolled steadily from the 13th-century tower. In the Palace chapel Princess Grace lay in state in a velvet-lined coffin. Still beautiful in death, with her face miraculously unmarked and her hair piled above her forehead, she was in a high-collared dress of white lace and had a favourite rosary of beads entwined in her fingers.

Only the citizens of Monaco were allowed to file past and pay their last respects. Outside, they bought bunches of flowers to bring her. Then, grief-stricken and in a state of shock, they shuffled through the dim chapel in a steady flow, pausing to bow or curtsey at the foot of the coffin. Police, speaking in whispers, turned away outsiders who tried to join the queue.

In the hospital, Stephanie had recovered enough to be told that her mother was dead. But she was

clearly too ill to attend the funeral, her damaged neck having been secured with a steel brace. Rainier and his other children withdrew into the Palace.

Tributes and messages of sympathy began pouring in. From Balmoral in Scotland, where she was on holiday, Queen Elizabeth sent a private personal message to Prince Rainier, and it was immediately arranged that Diana, Princess of Wales, would fly out to represent her at the funeral. In Washington President Reagan expressed his shock and sorrow at her "tragic and untimely death." In Philadelphia the Mayor, William Green, proclaimed, "She was, and is, Philadelphia's once-and-always first lady." Many former colleagues of stage and screen spoke lovingly of her. "She was sweet, beautiful, and gentle," said Gina Lollobrigida in Rome. "She was a real lady," said Gene Kelly. "She was also a regular sport and a fine actress." To Mickey Rooney, her co-star in *The Bridges at Toko-Ri*, her death meant the "terrible loss of a close, dear friend."

As preparations for her funeral were put in hand, the truth about the crash was finally established. Princess Stephanie had *not* been driving, but when the car had started to veer about the road she had leant across to grapple with the wheel and tried to pull on the handbrake. The Palace admitted that no fault had been discovered in the car, and the British Leyland engineers returned to England without having seen it. The doctors were exonerated of any blame. No treatment, however sophisticated, could have saved Grace.

On Thursday and Friday, as the initial shock wore off, the people of Monaco began to realise how much they had lost. Many felt suddenly desolate: their warm, regal yet maternal figurehead, who had conferred such respectability on Monaco, had been snatched from them. Where would they stand without her magnetic presence, her energy, and her blunt Irish stubbornness? On a more mercenary level, would the stream of big-spending transatlantic visitors, drawn by the presence of the American Princess, now dry up?

Her funeral took place on Saturday, September 18th. From all over the world they came to say farewell to her in the white stone Cathedral, where she had been married with such splendour twenty-six years before: royalty, heads of state, actors and actresses, family and friends. (One person not present was her mother, who was too ill even to be told of her daughter's death.) For many of the congregation there was a disconcerting sense of *déjà vu*: the same church, the same faces.

Among the mourners were the Princess of Wales, fulfilling with solemn dignity her first public engagement alone since the birth of her son; Nancy

Eyes shut, Prince Rainier follows the coffin in solemn procession, flanked by Caroline and Albert.

Reagan, wife of the American President, whose friendship with Grace dated back to Hollywood days thirty years earlier; and Danielle Mitterand, wife of the French President, who had himself been General de Gaulle's representative at the wedding.

Royal visitors included Prince Bernhardt of the Netherlands, Queen Sophia of Spain, Prince Bertil of Sweden, and Prince Philip of that other pocket-sized principality, Liechtenstein. Film stars included her old friends and leading men Frank Sinatra, Bob Hope and Cary Grant.

It was a calm, sunny autumn morning. The narrow streets were eerily silent until a fanfare of trumpets heralded the funeral procession. The Princess's ebony coffin, draped in a white standard bearing the Grimaldi arms and motto *Deo Juvante*

(''With God's Help''), was lifted from the chapel in the Palace where she had lain in state. It was carried by a dozen members of the Order of Penitents, with black capes over their habits, who bore it through the Palace gates to the beat of a muffled drum. Close behind walked Rainier, his silver head bowed, accompanied by Caroline and Albert. Caroline wore unrelieved black, from the lace mantilla covering her head to her plain shoes. Albert's red-and-white Order of St. Charles provided the only splash of colour in the sombre family group. The two children walked shoulder-to-shoulder with their father, so close that at times they seemed to support him physically.

When the pall-bearers set the coffin down in the cobbled square between the Palace and the

Cathedral, Rainier and the children stood stiffly at attention during the long pause needed for the rest of the mourners to file past, saluting the coffin, and take their places in the Cathedral. At last the royal family was left alone with the priests and pall-bearers and the red-plumed guard of honour.

The standard was folded and removed from the top of the coffin. As the voices of the choir soared into the anthem *Give unto them rest, O Lord, and let perpetual light shine upon them*, the bearers lifted their burden once more and carried it up the steep white steps to the Cathedral.

There it was placed before the altar. Rainier and his children sat on red velvet-backed chairs, with Grace's brother and two sisters from America immediately behind them.

The music for the Requiem Mass was a solemn mixture of Bach and Haydn interspersed with Gregorian Chant. It was sung by a hundred-voice choir, including Les Petits Chanteurs de Monaco, to whom Grace had given unstinting encouragement. A passage from Fauré's Requiem was played by the Monte Carlo Philharmonic Orchestra. As the notes floated up to the lofty ceiling, tears ran unchecked down the faces of Rainier and Caroline. Only Albert managed to contain his grief behind a set, outwardly-impassive mask. Many of the congregation wept openly, as the long, powerful, *Adagio for Strings* by the American composer Samuel Barber was played, and through the probing, inquisitive eye of the television camera the scene was intolerably moving. Never had grief been portrayed so starkly on the screen. No one who saw it will forget the sight of Rainier, stricken and bowed, with Caroline leaning pitifully towards him on one side, and Albert standing slim, young and brave on the other.

"We weep for our Princess Grace," said the Archbishop, Mgr. Charles Brand. "The brutal suddenness of her death accentuates our sorrow. . . When she was among us, our Princess was always ready to help those who needed it. Now it is time for her, in return, to receive the help afforded by our prayers."

He spoke not only for the congregation, but also for the countless people who had known and loved Grace in her many roles as actress, wife, mother, princess, benefactor, or merely friend.

After the mass, the coffin was taken to the Chapel of the Princes behind the High Altar, and in a private ceremony a few hours later she was buried in the Royal Vault.

Outside, in the sunny yet desolate streets, one ordinary citizen's remark summed up what his compatriots were feeling. "Monaco was empty before she came," he said, "and now it's empty again."

The shock of Princess Grace's death reverberated round the world in front-page headlines.

Previous page

"Many of the congregation wept openly, and through the probing, inquisitive eye of the television camera, the scene was intolerably moving."

The tragedy gave many magazines emotive front covers.

The life of Her Serene Highness

1929 November 12th. Born in Philadelphia.
1935 Grace's father runs for Mayor of Philadelphia, but fails.
1936 Goes to Ravenhill School, Philadelphia.
1941 First stage appearance, in *Don't Feed the Animals.*
1944 Goes to Stevens Academy in Germanstown, Philadelphia.
1946 Jack ("Kell") Kelly runner-up in Diamond Sculls at Henley Regatta.
1947 June-July. Kell wins Diamond Sculls at Henley Regatta. Grace to England to watch him.
Autumn. Goes to American Academy of Dramatic Arts, New York, living in Barbizon Hotel.
1948 Works as photographic model in New York.
1949 Spring. Joins Bucks County Playhouse, New Hope, Pennsylvania.
Summer. Kell wins Diamond Sculls again easily at Henley Regatta.
November 16th. Broadway debut in *The Father* at the Cort Theatre.
1950 Summer. Joins Elitch's Garden Theatre, Denver. First TV role in *Bethel Merriday.* Cast for *Fourteen Hours.* Autumn. Cast for *High Noon.* Signs seven-year contract with MGM.
Christmas. In *Alexander* (play) in Albany, New York.
1951 March. *Fourteen Hours* released. Television work; 60 - 80 plays and shows.
1952 Summer. In *To Be Continued* (play) at the Booth Theatre, New York.
1953 Summer. *High Noon* released. In Africa to make *Mogambo.* In *The Moon is Blue* (play) at Philadelphia's Playhouse in the Park.
September. *Mogambo* released. Makes *Dial M for Murder, Rear Window, The Country Girl, The Bridges at Toko-Ri* and *Green Fire.*
1954 Above five films released.
Makes *To Catch a Thief* for Paramount.
December. Chosen Best Actress by film critics. Suspended by MGM for refusing parts.
1955 March 30th. Academy Award (Oscar) for Best Actress of 1954. Pronounced top feminine attraction in movies.
Visits French Riviera for location shots of *To Catch a Thief.*
May 6th. Visits Monaco and meets Prince Rainier.
September. Starts making *The Swan.*
To Catch a Thief released.
Christmas. Prince Rainier visits the Kellys in Philadelphia.
1956 January 4th. Named best-dressed American woman of 1955.
January 6th. Grace and Rainier announce their engagement.
February. Starts making *High Society.*
February 23rd. Grace and Marlon Brando win "Henrietta" awards as top film actors in world.
April 4th. Sails from New York in *Constitution.*
April 11th. *The Swan* released in America.
April 12th. Arrives in Monaco.

April 18th. Civil Wedding ceremony.
April 19th. Marriage service in Cathedral.
July 17th. *High Society* released.
Kell wins bronze medal in Olympic Games Sculling.
October 15th. Visits President Eisenhower.
1957 January 23rd. Princess Caroline born.
Prince Rainier buys Roc Agel farm,
April. Private audience with the Pope in Rome.
1958 March 14th. Prince Albert born.
May. Becomes President of Monaco Red Cross.
1961 May 24th. Lunch with President Kennedy at the White House.
June. Visits site of ancestral home at Westport, Co. Mayo, Eire.
July. Pilgrimage to Lourdes.
1962 Announces return to films with *Marnie* but soon retracts plan.
1963 Becomes Honorary President of The World Association of the Friends of Children.
Appears in TV film of Monaco.
1965 February 1st. Princess Stephanie born.
Creates Princess Grace Foundation in Monaco for arts and crafts.
1966 Founds Garden Club of Monaco.
1967 Loses fourth baby during tour of Canada.
1968 Re-opening of the refurbished casino with grand ball.
Takes part in London-Brighton vintage car run, in De Dion Bouton.
1969 Modern additions to Royal Palace completed.
November 12th. 40th Birthday Party.
1970 International Arts Festival in Monaco.
November 16th. Deputises for Noel Coward (ill) and introduces Charity Show at Festival Hall, London.
1971 June. At Frank Sinatra's retirement show in Los Angeles.
October. Travels to Persepolis for Persia's 2,500th anniversary celebrations.
1974 Silver Jubilee of Prince Rainier's accession.
April 29th. Appears on-stage at New York's Lincoln Centre in tribute to Alfred Hitchcock.
1976 Joins Board of Twentieth Century-Fox.
September 6th. First Poetry-reading appearance, at Edinburgh Festival.
1977 Appears as Narrator in documentary film *The Children of Theatre Street.*
1978 Poetry-reading at the Aldeburgh Festival, Suffolk.
February. Poetry reading tour of US cities.
1979 November 12th. Caroline marries Philippe Junot.
1980 50th Birthday.
Caroline and Junot separate.
My Book of Flowers published.
1981 March 16th. Last poetry-reading in England, at Chichester Festival Theatre, West Sussex.
April. Silver Wedding celebrations.
July. Private visit to Henley Regatta, where she presents prizes.
Appears in New York's *Night of 1,000 Stars.*
1982 September 13th. Injured in car crash in morning.
September 14th. Dies at 9.30 pm.
September 18th. State Funeral in Monaco.

Filmography

Fourteen Hours
20th Century-Fox, 1951
Black and white; 92 minutes

Producer, Sol C. Siegel; *director,* Henry Hathaway; *screenplay,* John Paxton; *art directors,* Lyle Wheeler, Leland Fuller; *music,* Alfred Newman; *camera,* Joe MacDonald; *editor,* Dorothy Spencer.

Paul Douglas (Dunnigan); Richard Basehart (Robert Cosick); Barbara Bel Geddes (Virginia); Debra Paget (Ruth); Agnes Moorehead (Mrs Cosick); Robert Keith (Mr Cosick); Howard Da Silva (Lieutenant Moksar); Jeffrey Hunter (Danny); Martin Gabel (Dr Strauss); Grace Kelly (Mrs Fuller); Frank Faylen (Waiter); Jeff Corey (Sergeant Farley); James Millican (Sergeant Boyle); Donald Randolph (Dr Benson); Willard Waterman (Mr Harris); Kenneth Harvey (Police Operator); George MacQuarrie (Evangelist); Ann Morrison (Mrs Dunnigan); Forbes Murray (Police Commissioner); George Putnam (Radio Announcer); Ossie Davis, David Burns, Henry Slate, Harvey Lembeck, Lou Polan (Cab Drivers); Brad Dexter, Shep Menken (Reporters); Joyce Van Patten (Barbara); George Baxter (Attorney).

High Noon
United Artists, 1952
Black and white; 85 minutes

Producer, Stanley Kramer; *director,* Fred Zinnemann; *based on the story* "The Tin Star" by John W. Cunningham; *screenplay,* Carl Foreman; *music* Dmitri Tiomkin; *song,* Tiomkin, Ned Washington; *song sung by* Tex Ritter; *art director,* Rudolph Sternad; *set decorator,* Emmett Emerson; *sound,* Jean Speak; *camera,* Floyd Crosby; *editors,* Elmo Williams, Harry Gerstad.

Gary Cooper (Will Kane); Thomas Mitchell (Jonas Henderson); Lloyd Bridges (Harvey Pell); Katy Jurado (Helen Ramirez); Grace Kelly (Amy Kane); Otto Kruger (Percy Mettrick); Lon Chaney, Jr. (Martin Howe); Henry "Harry" Morgan (William Fuller); Ian MacDonald (Frank Miller); Eve McVeagh (Mildred Fuller); Harry Shannon (Cooper); Lee Van Cleef (Jack Colby); Bob Wilke (James Pierce); Sheb Woolley (Ben Miller); Tom London (Sam); Ted Stanhope (Station Master); Larry Blake (Gillis); William Phillips (Barber); Jeanne Blackford (Mrs. Henderson); James Millican (Baker); Cliff Clark (Weaver); Ralph Reed (Johnny); William Newell (Drunk); Lucien Prival (Bartender); Guy Beach (Fred); Howland Chamberlin (Hotel Clerk); Virginia Christine (Mrs. Simpson); Morgan Farley (Minister); Virginia Farmer (Mrs. Fletcher); Jack Elam (Charlie): Paul Dubov (Scott); Harry Harvey (Coy); Tim Graham (Sawyer); Nolan Leary (Lewis); Tom Greenway (Ezra); John Doucette (Trumbull); Dick Elliott (Kibbee).

Mogambo
MGM, 1953
Colour; 115 minutes

Producer, Sam Zimbalist; *director,* John Ford; *based on the play by* Wilson Collison; *screenplay,* John Lee Mahin; *art director,* Alfred Junge; *costumes,* Helen Rose; *second unit directors,* Richard Rosson, Yakima Canutt, James C. Havens; *assistant directors,* Wingate Smith, Cecil Ford; *camera,* Robert Surtees, Frederick A. Young; *editor,* Frank Clarke.

Clark Gable (Victor Marswell); Ava Gardner (Eloise Y. Kelly); Grace Kelly (Linda Nordley); Donald Sinden (Donald Nordley); Philip Stainton (John Brown Pryce); Eric Pohlmann (Leon Boltchak); Laurence Naismith (Skipper); Denis O'Dea (Father Joseph); Asa Etula (Young Native Girl); Wagenia Tribe of Belgian Congo, Samburu Tribe of Kenya Colony, Bahaya Tribe of Tanganyika, M'Beri Tribe of French Equatorial Africa (Themselves).

Dial M for Murder
Warner Bros., 1954
Colour; 88 minutes

Producer/director, Alfred Hitchcock; *based on the play by* Frederick Knott; *screenplay*, Hitchcock; *sets*, Edward Carrere, George James Hopkins; *music/music director*, Dmitri Tiomkin; *costumes*, Moss Mabry; *sound*, Oliver S. Garretson; *camera*, Robert Burks; *editor*, Rudi Fehr.

Ray Milland (Tony Wendice); Grace Kelly (Margot Wendice); Robert Cummings (Mark Halliday); John Williams (Chief Inspector Hubbard); Anthony Dawson (Captain Swan Lesgate); Leo Britt (The Narrator); Patric Allen (Pearson); George Leigh (William); George Alderson (The Detective); Robin Hughes (A Police Sergeant); Alfred Hitchcock (Man in Photo).

Rear Window
Paramount, 1954
Colour; 112 minutes

Producer/director, Alfred Hitchcock; *based on the novelette by* Cornell Woolrich; *screenplay*, John Michael Hayes; *Technicolor consultant*, Richard Mueller; *art directors*, Hal Pereira, Joseph McMillan Johnson; *set decorators*, Sam Comer, Ray Mayer; *music*, Franz Waxman; *costumes*, Edith Head; *assistant director*, Herbert Coleman; *special effects*, John P. Fulton; *camera*, Robert Burks; *editor*, George Tomasini.

James Stewart (L.B. "Jeff" Jeffries); Grace Kelly (Lisa Fremont); Wendell Corey (Thomas J. Doyle); Thelma Ritter (Stella); Raymond Burr (Lars Thorwald); Judith Evelyn (Miss Lonely Hearts); Ross Bagdasarian (Song Writer); Georgine Darcy (Miss Torso); Sara Berner (Woman on Fire Escape); Frank Cady (Fire Escape Man); Jesslyn Fax (Miss Hearing Aid); Rand Harper (Honeymooner); Irene Winston (Mrs. Thorwald); Harris Davenport (Newlywed); Marla English, Kathryn Grant (Party Girls); Edwin Parker, Fred Graham (Stunt Detectives); Harry Landers (Young Man); Bess Flowers (Woman with Poodle); James A. Cornell (Man).

The Country Girl
Paramount, 1954
Black and white; 104 minutes

Producers, William Perlberg, George Seaton; *director*, Seaton; *based on the play by* Clifford Odets; *assistant director*, Francisco Day; *musical sequences staged by* Robert Alton; *music*, Victor Young; *songs*, Ira Gershwin and Harold Arlen; *art director*, Hal Pereira; *camera*, John F. Warren; *editor*, Ellsworth Hoagland.

Bing Crosby (Frank Elgin); Grace Kelly (Georgie Elgin); William Holden (Bernie Dodd); Anthony Ross (Phil Cook); Gene Reynolds (Larry); Jacqueline Fontaine (Singer/Actress); Eddie Ryder (Ed); Robert Kent (Paul Unger); John W. Reynolds (Henry Johnson); Ida Moore, Ruth Rickaby (Women); Frank Scannell (Bartender); Richard Keene, Jack Kenney, Hal K. Dawson (Actors); Bob Alden (Bellboy); Neva Gilbert

(Lady); Chester Jones (Ralph, the Dresser); Jonathan Provost (Jimmie).

The Bridges at Toko-Ri
Paramount, 1954
Colour; 102 minutes

Producers, William Perlberg, George Seaton; *director*, Mark Robson; *based on the novel by* James A. Michener; *screenplay*, Valentine Davies; *music*, Lyn Murray; *art directors*, Hal Pereira, Henry Bumstead; *costumes*, Edith Head; *Technicolor consultant*, Richard Mueller; *makeup*, Wally Westmore; *technical advisor*, Commander M.U. Beebe, USN; *sound*, Hugo Grenzbach, Gene Garvin; *camera*, Loyal Griggs; *aerial camera*, Charles G. Clarke; *second unit camera*, Wallace Kelley, Thomas Tutweiler; *editor*, Alma Macrorie.

William Holden (Lieutenant Harry Brubaker); Grace Kelly (Nancy Brubaker); Fredric March (Rear Admiral George Tarrant); Mickey Rooney (Mike Forney); Robert Strauss (Beer Barrel); Charles McGraw (Commander Wayne Lee); Keiki Awaji (Kimiko); Earl Holliman (Nestor Gamidge); Richard Shannon (Lieutenant [S.G.] Olds); Willis Bouchey (Captain Evans); Dennis Weaver (Air Intelligence Officer); Marshall Beebe (Pilot); Cheryl Lynn Callaway (Susie); Nadene Ashdown (Kathey Brubaker); Jack Roberts (Quartermaster); Paul Kruger (Captain parker); Corey Allen, Jim Cronan (Enlisted Men); Bill Ash (Spotter).

Green Fire
MGM, 1954
Colour; 100 minutes

Producer, Armand Deutsch; *director*, Andrew Marton; *screenplay*, Ivan Goff, Ben Roberts; *art directors*, Cedric Gibbons, Malcolm Brown; *camera*, Paul Vogel; *editor*, Harold F. Kress.

Stewart Granger (Rian X. Mitchell); Grace Kelly (Catherine Knowland); Paul Douglas (Vic Leonard); John Ericson (Donald Knowland); Murvyn Vye (El Moro); Jose Torvay (Manuel); Robert Tafur (Father Ripero); Joe Dominguez (Jose); Nacho Galindo (Officer Perez); Charlita (Dolores); Natividad Vacio (Hernandez); Rico Alaniz (Antonio); Paul Marion (Roberto); Bobby Dominguez (Juan); Charles Stevens, Joe Herrera (Bandits); Martin Garralaga (Gonzales); Alberto Morin (Carlos); Rudolfo Hoyos, Jr. (Pedro, the Bartender); Lillian Molieri (Mexican Girl); Marie Delgado, Juli Loffredo, Frances Dominguez, Tina Menard (Women).

To Catch a Thief
Paramount, 1955
Colour; 97 minutes

Producer/director, Alfred Hitchcock; *based on the novel by* David Dodge; *screenplay*, John Michael Hayes; *second unit director*, Herbert Coleman; *art directors*, Hall Pereira, Joseph MacMillan Johnson; *set decorators*, Sam Comer, ARthur Krams; *music*, Lyn Murray; *assistant director*, Daniel McCauley; *costumes*, Edith head; *Technicolor consultant*, Richard Mueller; *sound*, Lewis and John Cope; *special effects*, John P. Fulton; *process camera*, Farciot Edouart; *camera*, Robert Burks; *second unit camera*, Wallace Kelley; *editor*, George Tomasini.

Cary Grant (John Robie); Grace Kelly (Frances Stevens); Jessie Royce Landis (Mrs. Stevens); John Williams (H.H. Hughson); Charles Vanel (Bertani); Brigitte Auber (Danielle); Jean Martinelli (Foussard); Georgette Anys (Germaine); Roland Lesaffre (Claude); Jean Hebey (Mercier); Rene

Blancard (Lepic); Wee Willie Davis (Big Man in Kitchen); Edward Manouk (Kitchen Help); Russell Gaige (Mr. Sanford); Marie Stoddard (Mrs. Sanford); Paul "Tiny" Newlan (Vegetable Man in Kitchen); Alfred Hitchcock (Solemn Bus Passenger); Loulette Sablon, Nina Borget (Frenchwomen); Barry Norton, Cosmo Sardo (Frenchmen); George A. Nardelli, George Paris (Croupiers); Philip Van Zandt (Jewelry Clerk); Steven Geray (Desk Clerk); Adele St. Maur (Woman with Bird Cage).

The Swan
MGM, 1956
Colour; 112 minutes

Producer, Dore Schary; *director*, Charles Vidor; *based on the play by* Ferenc Molnar; *screenplay*, John Dighton; *art directors*, Cedric Gibbons, Randall Duell; *music*, Bronislau Kaper; *costumes*, Helen Rose; *assistant director*, Ridgeway Callow; *camera*, Joseph Ruttenberg, Robert Surtees; *editor*, John Dunning.

Grace Kelly (Princess Alexandra); Alec Guinness (Prince Albert); Louis Jourdan (Dr. Nicholas Agi); Agnes Moorehead (Queen Maria Dominika); Jessie Royce Landis (Princess Beatrix); Brian Aherne (Father Hyacinth); Leo G. Carroll (Caesar); Estelle Winwood (Symphorosa); Van Dyke Parks (George); Christopher Cook (Arsene); Robert Coote (Captain Wunderlich); Doris Lloyd (Countess Sigenstoyn); Edith Barrett (Beatrix's Maid).

High Society
MGM, 1956
Colour; 107 minutes

Producer, Sol C. Siegel; *director*, Charles Walters; *based on the play The Philadelphia Story* by Philip Barry; *screenplay*, John Patrick; *songs*, Cole Porter; *music supervisors/adaptors*, Johnny Green, Saul Chaplin; *music director*, Green; *orchestrators*, Conrad Salinger, Nelson Riddle; *additional orchestrators*, Robert Franklyn, Albert Senrey; *music numbers staged by* Charles Walters; *art directors*, Cedric Gibbons, Hans Peters; *set decorators*, Edwin B. Willis, Richard Pefferle; *costumes*, Helen Rose; *makeup*, William Tuttle; *recording supervisor*, Dr. Wesley C. Miller; *assistant director*, Arvid Griffen; *special effects*, A. Arnold Gillespie; *camera*, Paul C. Vogel; *editor*, Ralph E. Winters.

Bing Crosby (C.K. Dexter-Haven); Grace Kelly (Tracy Lord); Frank Sinatra (Mike Connor); Celeste Holm (Liz Imbrie); John Lund (George Kittredge); Louis Calhern (Uncle Willie); Sidney Blackmer (Seth Lord); Margalo Gillmore (Mrs. Seth Lord); Louis Armstrong (Himself); Lydia Reed (Caroline Lord); Gordon Richards (Dexter-Haven's Butler); Richard Garrick (Lord's Butler); Richard Keene (Mac); Ruth Lee, Helen Spring (Matrons); Paul Keast (Editor); Reginald Simpson (Uncle Willie's Butler); Hugh Boswell (Parson).

The Children of Theatre Street
Peppercorn-Wormser, 1977
Colour; 90 minutes

Producer, Earle Mack; *associate producer*, Jean Dalrymple; *directors*, Robert Dornhelm, Mack; *screenplay*, Beth Gutcheon; *artistic director*, Oleg Briansky; *camera*, Karl Kofler; *editor*, Tina Frese. Princess Grace (Narrator); featuring the students and faculty of the Vaganova Choreographic Institute, including: Angelina Armeiskaya, Alec Timoushin, Lena Voronzova, Michaela Cerna, and Galina Messenzeva; and Konstantine Zaklinsky of the Kirov Ballet.